Night Fishing in Galilee

The Journey Toward Spiritual Wisdom

Kenneth Arnold

COWLEY PUBLICATIONS

Cambridge, Massachusetts

Library of Congress Cataloging-in-Publication Data:
Arnold, Kenneth.
   Night fishing in Galilee : the journey toward spiritual
   wisdom / Kenneth Arnold.
         p.   cm.
Includes bibliographical references.
   ISBN 1–56101–195–9 (pbk. : alk. paper)
   1. Bible. N.T. John—Meditations. I. Title.
   BS2615.4 .A77 2002
   248.8'4—dc21

                                        2002005166

Scripture quotations are taken from *The New Revised Standard Version* of the Bible, ©1989, by the Division of Christian Education of the National Council of the Churches of Christ in the United States of America. Used by permission.

Cover art: *Moonlit Seascape*, about 1883; John La Farge, American (1835–1910) Transparent and opaque watercolor on paper; Sheet: 16.99 × 12.22 cm (6¹¹⁄₁₆ × 4¹³⁄₁₆ in.) Bequest of Miss Mary C. Wheelwright, 59.688. Courtesy, Museum of Fine Arts, Boston. Reproduced with permisson. ©2002 Museum of Fine Arts, Boston. All Rights Reserved.

This book was printed in the United States of America on acid-free paper.

Cowley Publications
907 Massachusetts Avenue
Cambridge, Massachusetts 02139
800–225–1534 • *www.cowley.org*

FOR CONNIE

in this world and the next

Cowley Publications is a ministry of the Society of Saint John the Evangelist, a religious community of men in the Episcopal Church. Emerging from the Society's tradition of prayer, theological reflection, and diversity of mission, the press is centered in the rich heritage of the Anglican Communion.

Cowley Publication seeks to provide books, audio cassettes, CDs, and other resources for the ongoing theological exploration and spiritual development of the Episcopal Church and others in the body of Christ. To this end, it is dedicated to developing a new generation of theological writers, encouraging them to produce timely, creative, and stimulating publications of excellence, and making these publications available widely, reaching both clergy and lay persons.

Contents

Acknowledgements

The seed for this book was planted with an offhand remark by my former spiritual director, Clair McPherson, one afternoon in his office in New Rochelle, New York. We were complaining about the church, and he said something about how we need to discover what it means to be adult Christians. Later, when I was reading John 21 in connection with a sermon I was writing, I suddenly saw in that chapter a model for becoming spiritually mature. It all seemed immediately clear. It took me another two years to work out the schema, but I never would have seen it had the seed not been there.

Cynthia Shattuck, former managing director of Cowley Publications and a friend of many years, guided me through the process of making book sense of my ideas. She made me rewrite the whole book when I thought it was perfect, and she edited the next draft with a deft hand. The authors with whom she worked over the more than two decades she helped shape Cowley

Publications into a force for spiritual good in the church are in her debt; the church is in her debt. This book, and nearly two hundred others, would not exist without her skill and selfless care.

There are more people than I can name who have helped me along my own journey toward spiritual wisdom. Those I mention here seem especially important to me in regard to this book: Michael Becker, Robert Brashear, Kenneth Burton, Barbara Crafton, Elizabeth Edman, James Ismael Ford, Sheila Gordon, Frank T. Griswold, Scott Holland, Katherine Kurs, Bill Lent, Catherine Madsen, Stephanie Mitchem, Wendell Meyer, Scott O'Brien, Joe Pace, Randi Rashkover, Johnny Ross, Hal Taussig, and Debra Wagner; the people of St. Mary's and St. Clement's Episcopal Churches in New York City, the people of West Park Presbyterian Church in New York, the deacons of the Diocese of New York (especially the "cranks"), and Lyndon Harris and the people at St. Paul's Chapel New York. Timothy Morehouse, Clarke Bell, Eileen Walsh, and Michael Bacon were particularly important to my spiritual growth during the writing of this book. Norman McNatt taught me to fly fish on the South Branch of the Raritan River.

My children, Nick and Ruth, continue to amaze me as their journeys unfold. My wife, Connie Kirk, has helped me to understand what I have been wanting to say for so many years. She is the vitality of this book and of my life, the greatest and most surprising gift of wisdom in this journey.

Introduction to the Journey

You may have reached that spiritual stage in life that Hinduism describes as "forest-dwelling," no longer what is known as a householder. Your children are young adults and you are established in your career. People frequently look to you for answers to the big questions, and, somewhat to your surprise, you often know what to say to them. You have become spiritually mature. Your sense of the divine is clear, although still evolving, and your understanding of the vocation you bear is full. You have nothing to prove. As a forest-dweller you have time to reflect on who you are and where you are going. You can afford to be contemplative but have not yet renounced the world. That comes later. In my own case, I still live in the city and go every day to an office, but spiritually I am in the forest (preferably near a trout stream), which is a metaphor for dwelling in God's presence.

Everyone is able spiritually to attain that same condition of maturity. It is part of our soul's life cycle—but like old age, not everyone gets there. The difficulty

is that we twenty-first-century people are not accustomed to think about ourselves as either spiritually
mature or immature, at least not as much as we think
about being in or out of shape physically. We might
seek spiritual experiences through yoga or worship or
music because we want to feel better (or feel better
about ourselves). These uplifting moments are only
fleetingly pleasurable, however; they are not the same
as the deeper dimensions of spiritual experience that,
like regular physical exercise, affect the long-term
health of the whole being. If diet and exercise condition physical health and longevity, what contributes to
spiritual wisdom? What can we do to avoid remaining
the spiritual equivalents of twelve-year-olds?

This book is about attaining spiritual maturity, an
extended biblical reflection on what it means to grow
into theological adulthood. The story that will guide
our thinking is the twenty-first chapter of the Gospel
of John. Its primary characters are the apostle Peter and
the unnamed Beloved Disciple; the author is an
unknown disciple who is telling the story to Christian
believers. With the disciples in this story, Christians are
part of a church that is like a fishing boat. The meaning of the story is not always clear, in the ways that
many biblical stories are unclear; like the experience of
being in a boat on the water at night, the narrative can
be disorienting, even frightening. One of the chal-
lenges we face as hearers of the story today is that we
were not there, we do not know as much as its first
hearers knew about recent history, and we are not
steeped in the Hebrew Scriptures as they were. By
reading the story carefully and imaginatively, however,
I hope to clarify its meaning for those of us who were
not fishing with Peter and the Beloved Disciple on the

Sea of Tiberias and to uncover the value of this story
for our own spiritual coming of age.

The author of the Gospel of John tells a version of
the Jesus story that embodies the life and beliefs of a
particular Christian community at the end of the first
century of the common era. This community revered
as its founder an otherwise unnamed Beloved Disciple
and modeled its communal life on what its members
saw as his intimate relationship with Jesus. They felt
that they were being actively led in this spiritual path
by the Holy Spirit, who inspired the Gospel of John.
Underlying the community's message in this story may
also be a political conflict between the followers of the
Beloved Disciple and those of the apostle Peter, which
reflect two very different visions of the church, one
hierarchical and orderly in its structure and the other
small and communitarian.[1] Conflict between Peter and
the Beloved Disciple pervades John's entire gospel and
may lie at the heart of Chapter 21, as indeed the conflict their points of view represent was at the center of
Church struggles for identity and order throughout the
first four centuries of its life. The Community of the
Beloved Disciple described in John's Gospel did not
survive these struggles.

In this book, I interpret the message of John 21 for
Christians and other seekers who do not know how, or

1. I owe this insight to Raymond Brown, in *The Community of the Beloved
Disciple: The Life, Loves, and Hates of an Individual Church in New Testament
Times* (New York: Paulist Press, 1979), pp. 81-88. It also appears later in
Wes Howard-Brook's *Becoming Children of God: John's Gospel and Radical Discipleship* (Maryknoll, NY: Orbis Books, 1994), p. 475. Both of these books
have provided important background information. Howard-Brook's reading of the Gospel of John has been especially valuable in many ways. His
chapter on John 21 has frequently been suggestive. Indeed, the very title
of this book is indebted to the title of chapter 29 in his, "Fishing at Night
in Galilee."

sometimes even what, to believe at the beginning of the
third millennium. I read it as a prophetic message to
the church of the first century as well as our own: the
future belongs not to an institution but, as John's community insists, to the witnesses who encounter the living Christ. The gospel of John draws on the story of
the people of Israel, the wisdom tradition of the
Hebrew Scriptures, and its own encounter with the living Christ to offer a radical vision of life in the Spirit.
This book uses the lessons of John 21 to teach us about
the inner life of our journey toward the Wisdom of
God in whose presence we might lead enlightened,
adult lives in faithful community.

In order to do this I have divided John 21 into six
sections, each of which signifies one dimension of this
journey, beginning with isolation and moving through
discernment, transformation, vocation, freedom, and
wisdom. These dimensions of faith (or discipleship)
are not like stages of growth, as if one were progress-
ing from one to the next—although we want to be
people who dwell in wisdom rather than isolation—but
spiritual locales through which we move and to which
on many occasions we return. Our cumulative experience forms our spiritual selves, and our formation is
never complete. We are always works in progress. In
each of these dimensions, as we will see in my reading
of John 21, we mature through a life-long process of
biblical understanding, spiritual practice, community
formation, and grace.

The story in John 21 is one of the best-known resurrection appearances of Jesus—and the most narra-
tively rich. In it, the risen Jesus appears at dawn on the
shore of the Sea of Tiberias (known in the other
gospels as the Sea of Galilee) after the disciples have

spent a fruitless night fishing. They catch one hundred and fifty-three fish when he tells them where to set their nets. The Beloved Disciple then recognizes Jesus. Peter jumps into the water and swims to shore, where Jesus is broiling a fish on a charcoal fire. He invites the disciples to join him for breakfast once they have hauled in the miraculous catch. After they have eaten, Jesus asks Peter three times if he loves him—and when Peter replies each time that he does, instructs him to feed Jesus' sheep. Jesus then tells Peter that he will be taken where he does not wish to go (to a death like Jesus') and says to him, "Follow me." When Peter notices that the Beloved Disciple is following behind them, he asks, "What about him?" What is to become of this other favorite? Jesus replies that it is not Peter's concern. "You follow me."

John 21 is a rite of passage. It begins when Peter and the other disciples on an isolated shore enter a dark night of the soul. They pass through waters, in which (as in baptism) they encounter death with Jesus but are, like him, raised to abundance. On another shore they encounter the resurrection life, which begins the path to spiritual maturity. The essence of transformation from a culture of death to life is revealed to them in prayer, scripture, community, service, and the teachings of Jesus. Like these disciples, we are called in life-altering encounter with the risen Christ to be in the world with others and to care for them. In that understanding of Christian vocation, the miraculous catch of fish is not about converting others: we do not capture and eat those who are not Christian. It is about being with others, inviting them to Jesus' open table fellowship, which welcomes all to the feast. As followers of Jesus, we find our way through the Christ to life in wisdom.

metaphors

My approach to John 21 is to read it in the crucible of my own experience, not to try to find out what the chapter *really* means or what *actually* happened. Both are lost to us. In scripture, we enter the playground of the Spirit where God speaks to us directly in creative encounter. Reading the Bible—or any sacred text—in this way is an act of imagination. Although we begin with the story itself, we deliberately investigate meaning beyond the boundaries of both narrative and doctrine. It may be one of the few ways in which we can still read sacred texts in the twenty-first century.

In my first encounter with it, this story was important for my own spiritual growth. It was the medium through which God called me to ministry. I did not know the depths of what I was being called to do at the time. When we encounter God, we often think we are being asked to *do* something. I certainly did. But I was actually being invited to come to know and ultimately *become* my deeper self. That is an ongoing project. It is not only about my spiritual identity; it is about encountering and being changed in the divine wisdom. Spiritual maturity is about coming to understand that life in the Spirit is not about me.

My journey begins, as it did for these disciples, in an encounter with the resurrected Christ. I was on retreat at a monastery on the Hudson River in New York State. On Friday in Easter Week, swept away by the holiness of it all, I woke before dawn to go down to the river to meditate and watch the sun rise. With me I had a prayer book and a Bible, still unaware that the gospel reading for that day was from John 21, which cries out to be read by water. The rocky shore of the Hudson was perfect. After reading the passage, I closed my eyes, facing east to await the warmth of the sun to spill over the hills across the water. There was still a chill in the air; the rock I sat on sucked the warmth out of me. I wondered if I would last until sunrise. I was not accustomed to ascetic practices. Suddenly I heard fish feeding—quick splashes that made me wish I had brought a fishing rod. In retrospect, I think they must have been striped bass, which years later I learned to catch at night on the Rhode Island shore. Even that far up river, beyond Poughkeepsie at Hyde Park, the Hudson is tidal—that morning the river flowed north—and bass might well have been up there. I did not open my eyes to look, feeling virtuously like one who has resisted a powerful temptation, although my mind was busy fishing. When the sun rose, however, I quickly looked but saw no evidence of fish. Down the river was a sailboat unlike any I had ever seen, except in photographs of the Nile. It had what is known as a lateen sail sharply triangled across the bow. The sail was deep red, the boat angling across the river directly toward me. In disbelief, I closed my eyes. When I opened them a few minutes later, the boat was gone.

Immediately and oddly, I felt that I had experienced the presence of the living Christ. His presence told me that as I was being fed on the Hudson shore, so I was to go and feed others. I was to "fish for people," as were the disciples called by Jesus in Luke's Gospel. Although I wanted to run through the corridors of the monastery shouting, "Christ is risen!" I did nothing of the sort. Instead, I interpreted this experience as an invitation to explore ordination in the Episcopal Church and to become an expert angler. I am as passionate about fishing as I am about the church. There was a time, in fact, when I went fishing two or three times a week and attended church only once. Now the pattern is reversed.

God is in both activities, as the first disciples of Jesus came to understand.

Fishing is, of course, an ancient and rich image for spiritual inquiry. Night fishing is almost mystical in its intensity—and depending on the fish one is seeking can be the most rewarding. It is most productive to fish at night on the Sea of Galilee. Striped bass are best fished for at night or in the darkness just before dawn. The big trout come out to feed after sundown when every cast might also snag a bat. Night fishing is not without its terrors. I have stood in a salt water pond in Rhode Island and felt striped bass weighing thirty pounds bump against my legs, seen their quick bodies pouring in with the tide. And been unable to catch any of them. The dark night of the soul can be spiritually full and empty at the same time. Both require stumbling around in the water at night, slipping on rocks, losing one's way, going home empty handed. Every angler knows that what makes the difference in fishing, whether at night or in daylight, is not the equipment—the rod will not catch the fish, the boat is only a vehicle—but seeking to know the water and the fish. Fishing is only inquiry: the goal is to know not to kill and eat. Every good angler understands that truth. And so does every mature spiritual seeker.

"I'm Going Fishing"

1 After these things Jesus showed himself again to the disciples by the Sea of Tiberias; and he showed himself in this way. 2 Gathered there together were Simon Peter, Thomas called the Twin, Nathanael of Cana in Galilee, the sons of Zebedee, and two others of his disciples. 3 Simon Peter said to them, "I am going fishing." They said to him, "We will go with you." They went out and got into the boat, but that night they caught nothing.

The story of Jesus' death seems to be more firmly at the heart of the gospels than his teachings are. For the most part his last hours are the same in all of them: Jesus gathers with his disciples in a room in Jerusalem to eat together. This table fellowship is one of the distinctive characteristics of their common life. In Matthew, Mark, and Luke it becomes the basis for the Eucharist, enacted in memory of Jesus; in John, it is an opportunity for Jesus to speak at length about the meaning of his ministry and to wash the disciples' feet in a touching gesture of care. Despite what seems to be a close community of followers, Judas betrays him to the authorities and Peter denies that he knows Jesus. Not only Peter and Judas, but all of the disciples in these three accounts seem to desert Jesus once he is arrested. Jesus dies utterly alone, abandoned even by God, to whom he cries, "Why have your forsaken me?"

John's Gospel differs from these accounts in significant ways. It places Jesus' mother Mary, the Beloved Disciple, and a number of women at the foot of the cross. Of the key disciples, only this one remains as the symbol of faithful witness for the Johannine community. He does not appear in the other gospels. Although Judas betrays him, and Peter denies him, John's Jesus does not die alone. Not only that, after his death his body is protected and cared for. Joseph of Arimathea claims the body and properly prepares it for burial. John's community seems to understand the meaning of the death of Jesus differently from the other gospel communities. This Jesus dies not in isolation but in a family's care. The story of his death already assumes resurrection. John's Gospel is a resurrection story from beginning to end, not (as the others are) a Passion story with teachings and resurrection added. Significantly, the foot-washing act that Jesus performs at the Last Supper is about life-affirming care, not remembrance of the dead. It occurs only in John.

These very different visions of the death of Jesus both affirm, however, that death without God is a state of intolerable isolation. Those who deny and betray Jesus suffer deeply. In John, it is Peter who bears the burden of this life-denying isolation. He is the one who, in John 18:25-27, will deny that he knows Jesus, and then will be among the first to look into the empty tomb. That had to be a devastating moment, to stand in the mouth of the place where the body had been laid and to fail to understand what has happened. Peter is stuck with death. The Beloved Disciple peers in and believes. What does he believe?

To understand this gathering of disciples at the beginning of John 21, we need to look back with Peter into the empty tomb. When Mary Magdalene goes to the tomb, she finds that the stone has been rolled away. She goes immediately to tell Simon Peter and the Beloved Disciple that someone has stolen the body. Both disciples run to the tomb, the Beloved Disciple arriving first. Peter is the first to go inside, however. He enters the abyss, the place of death. Now Peter is in the tomb and Jesus is not. Although the disciples do not know it yet—"they did not understand the scripture, that he must rise from the dead"—Jesus is no longer in the isolation of the grave. Peter remains, however, among the dead. The Beloved Disciple, John says, believed. It is a touching moment. Both Peter and the Beloved Disciple turn around and return to their homes. They remain in ignorance. But Peter, who has no faith at this moment, is alone.

Peter has chosen his isolation by denying Jesus on the night before he was put to death. It is significant that in neither of the Johannine resurrection appearances preceding Chapter 21 is Peter mentioned by name: he has still not acknowledged, or been acknowledged by, the Risen One. If he is present and unnamed, it is surely because in the eyes of the writer of the gospel Peter still does not understand what has happened. He is not part of the community's reality. He remains, I think, in a kind of willful isolation that, in revealing himself by the Sea of Tiberias, Jesus breaks

where
who how

through. Another way to put it is that Peter finally chooses resurrection over death and isolation. The overriding message of John 21 is that all of us have the same choice.

The place where Jesus reveals himself to the disciples and cooks them breakfast is beside the Sea of Tiberias. The Spirit blows over waters. They are holy. These are the places in scripture where we are most likely to meet the Holy One—the ocean over which God hovers at creation, the Sea of Reeds crossed by the people of Israel as they flee Egypt, the great flood that destroys everything but one vessel with its living cargo, the deep into which the great fish takes Jonah, the Jordan where Jesus is baptized. The waters separate (but also join) devastation and renewal; they are shores of isolation and shores of wisdom. These are boundary waters. And like their counterpart, the desert, they are both dangerous and life-giving.

The Sea of Tiberias—as the Sea of Galilee is often called in the gospel of John—was the name given to it in the first century after Herod Antipas had built a town on the southwest shore and named it in honor of the Roman emperor, Tiberius. In Hebrew, the lake is known as Chinnereth (meaning "harp," after its shape), and in other biblical sources as Gennesaret. It is twelve to thirteen miles long and seven to eight miles wide. Although it is subject to strong winds and unusual weather, the setting is beautiful, blue water bounded by cliffs except in the north where the water meets green plains. The northwest hills hold some of the earliest prehistoric remains in Palestine.

The scene at the beginning of this chapter in John invites us into various realities, as the Bible always does. First, there is the emotional sense of things: how the disciples might have felt after the death of Jesus. This narrative reality is important. The story conveys the meaning not only through events but also through the feelings the events elicit in readers. The story of the life and death of Jesus is meant to lead us to certain conclusions. How the disciples feel in the aftermath of the crucifixion draws us toward our own encounter with the Risen One. The writer wants us to feel what they feel.

Second, the opening scene (and indeed the chapter itself) tell us something about the state of the early Christian church. The gospel accounts are as much about what is going on in the early church communities to which they are addressed as they are about supposedly historical events. Sometimes, the situation in the writer's environment is more important than history. Political truth can take precedence over narrative fealty. In the case of John 21, Jesus appears at a time of crisis in the community for which John was writing near the end of the first century. The nature of this crisis, which becomes clearer as the chapter unfolds, has to do with the underlying rivalry between Peter and the Beloved Disciple. The distinctive community of the Beloved Disciple views its relationship to Jesus very differently from that of the emerging institutional church that Peter represents. It is a vision that emphasizes a more personal, even mystical, mode of encounter with Jesus, as opposed to the institutional church of which Peter is the assumed leader. John's community feels it is in danger of disappearing.

Third, we as contemporary readers and interpreters of the story also affect its multiple meanings. The gospel writer, who is writing this account a generation or two later, looks back at the communities around Jesus and interprets their past and present each in the light of earlier Bible stories. We read the gospel of John today in the same way, in our own context and using our own imaginations to interpret it. The rabbis read the Torah in this way, imagining themselves to be part of the whole, even as participants in the story. The Bible reveals itself most deeply and most vividly when it is read in this way.

As a reader I can identify immediately with the emotional loss Peter and the other disciples must have felt as they stood on the once-familiar shore of the Sea of Tiberias after the crucifixion of Jesus. Although they have returned to the region they came from, a part of the country they know well, they may not experience the landscape in the same way they did when Jesus was alive with them in it. Its emotional texture has changed for them, just as a house changes after the death of someone who has lived in it a long time. In the presence of absence, one's very sense of self can alter. The scripture does not tell us that Peter and the disciples felt estranged from the shore they had known so well, but my own experience of loss suggests how they might have felt. Their subsequent failure to catch fish in waters they worked professionally is also a clue. All that we have in John 21 is Peter's announcement that he is going fishing and the reply from the others that they will go along. Nothing important is happening, there is nothing else to do. The lack of enthusiasm is also a sign, however, of their emotional state.

All Christians know from Matthew, Mark, and Luke that Peter was a fisherman who left his nets to follow Jesus. In fact, Luke's version of the story of the miraculous catch of fish (5:1-11) ends with a call to Simon and his fishing partners James and John, who have been out all night in Peter's boat, to stop their work and fish for people. Prior to Chapter 21, however, John does not identify Peter as a fisherman in his gospel. Nor is he a leader among the disciples. Instead of being called from his nets, he learns about Jesus second-hand from his brother Andrew (1:40-42), who was apparently one of the followers of John the Baptist. Furthermore, in this first encounter with Simon, Jesus inexplicably renames him Cephas, an Aramaic word for "rock," which translates to Peter (*petra*) in Greek.

Peter seldom appears after this in John, and when he does it is invariably in association with Judas, which suggests how John's community viewed him. In John 6:66-71, for example, Peter declares his allegiance to Jesus when others have deserted him, but Jesus responds by identifying one of those who remain as a traitor. In John 13, where Jesus washes the disciples' feet, Peter demurs but then agrees when Jesus says, "Unless I wash you, you have no share with me." Immediately after, Jesus makes a reference to Judas, saying "Not all of you are clean." Further on in this chapter, we read:

> Jesus was troubled in spirit, and declared, "Very truly, I tell you, one of you will betray me." The disciples looked at one another, uncertain of whom he was speaking. One of his disciples—the one whom Jesus loved—was reclining next to him; Simon Peter therefore motioned to him to ask Jesus of whom he was speaking (13:21-24).

It is at the end of this chapter, the most extensive treatment of Peter in John's Gospel, that Jesus tells Peter that he will deny him.

The next scene in which Peter appears is in the garden where Jesus is arrested. Judas arrives with a detachment of soldiers; Peter draws a sword and cuts off a slave's ear. Jesus rebukes him. Soon after, Peter goes into the courtyard of the high priest and denies Jesus three times, as predicted in Chapter 13. We hear no more about him until he and the Beloved Disciple race each other to look at the empty tomb. After Peter returns home, he disappears from the main story. So in John's Gospel Peter is consistently identified with Judas as one who has betrayed Jesus and his message. But the tradition of Peter as fisherman returns to the narrative in this chapter: when Peter announces that he is going fishing, we are to recall the fisherman and to understand that he is not going to be fishing recreationally. We are to understand that he is returning to something he used to do. Peter also returns to life.

Some have suggested that Peter and the disciples are going to catch not fish but converts, that this is a story of their carrying out the Great Commission. That is certainly possible. The message, in any case, is this: Peter does not know what he is doing. He and the disciples are simply going out there, and whether it is to catch fish or people is unimportant. They do not go as a community but rather, it seems, as a collection of isolated individuals. The church is not gathered here, only people lacking purpose and even hope. The result is perhaps predictable—they catch nothing. It is a long dull night. But the scripture tells us right away, before we even learn about Peter's fishing excursion, that something important will transpire. Jesus will reveal himself (God's glory will be made known as it was to Israel during its forty years of wandering in Sinai) to Peter and six others, most of whom are familiar to Christians.

Who are Peter's companions on the shore? Some are named: James, John, Thomas, and Nathanael. Two are unnamed, although we learn that one of them is the Beloved Disciple.

Although Peter is going fishing, we have no particular reason to associate the others named with the profession, except for John and James, the sons of Zebedee, and we have that information only from the other gospels, not from John. The three of them are from the town of Beth-saida on the other side of the lake where the Jordan flows in from the north. They have fished these waters. James and John left their boats and their father behind to follow Jesus, and both are associated with Jesus at critical points in his ministry—at the Transfiguration, for example. When they ask to be seated at the right and left hands of Jesus in his glory (Mark 10:37)—in Matthew, their mother, Salome, asks for preference on their behalf—Jesus promises only that they will suffer as he will suffer. Although they are clearly part of the inner circle in the these accounts, neither brother is mentioned by name in John.

Thomas the Twin may also be a Galilean. For Christians he is Doubting Thomas, the one who is skeptical that his friends have seen the Risen Christ: "Unless I see the mark of the nails in his hands, and put my finger in the mark of the nails and my hand in his side, I will not believe" (20:25). Thomas demands and receives this proof when Jesus appears to the disciples a second time, he then calls Jesus "my Lord and my God." In John 11:16, he is impetuous in declaring his willingness to follow Jesus when he says that he and the disciples are to go to see Lazarus, who has died, urging, "Let us also go, that we may die with him." Later he is confused when Jesus tells the disciples that they know where he is going: "Lord, we do not know where you are going. How can we know the way?" I picture him as young, an enthusiast who is then angry or embarrassed about the death of Jesus and its betrayal of expectations. Thomas is called the twin for unknown reasons, although the third-century *Acts of Thomas* suggests that he was literally Jesus' twin. Legend has it that he took Christianity to India, where there remains a community that claims him as its founder. But here on the shore of Tiberias he is, like the others, a witness who is unsure to whom he is to give testimony (or even what he is to testify).

Neither Thomas nor Nathanael appear in any of the other gospels. Nathanael comes from Cana, where Jesus performs the first "sign" of his ministry when he turns water into wine at a wedding. He is also the one who sarcastically asks, when told that Jesus is the Messiah, "Can anything good come out of Nazareth?" It is a scholar's question from one who knows that according to scripture the Messiah will not come from Galilee. Later, Jesus calls him "an Israelite in whom there is no deceit" because he will see Jesus as he truly is, the Glory of God. Despite his initial skepticism, Nathanael proclaims Jesus the Messiah, for which he is promised a vision of the Son of Man in glory (John 1:51). From John's perspective he is a representative disciple whose faith is confirmed in seeing Jesus.

The Beloved Disciple is different from the others named in this small group. He is intimate with Jesus in a way the others are not, as we see in John's account of the Last Supper, where he reclines against Jesus' breast. He also stands with Mary at the foot of the cross and takes her into his own home at the request of the dying Jesus, forming the symbolic new family of love exemplified by the Community of the Beloved Disciple. Furthermore, he is the one who "witnesses and has written these things" (v.24) and may have been the author of the gospel of John. Later on we will see that the conclusion of John 21 suggests that the Beloved Disciple has recently died: "The rumor spread in the community that this disciple would not die. Yet Jesus did not say to him that he would not die, but, 'If it is my will that he remain until I come, what is that to you?'" (21:23).

Most commentators think that the Beloved Disciple was a historical person who occupies in John an idealized or symbolic role as the quintessential disciple. He is a shadowy persona whom the author pairs with Peter throughout the Gospel of John, and he is the first to recognize Jesus when he appears on the shore. The two of them are exemplary figures who together are used by the author of John to raise important ecclesial and spiritual concerns about the nature of the believer's relationship with the Risen Christ. Most importantly, the Beloved Disciple represents the *sensibility* of John's community, which defines its identity distinctively in terms of its close personal relationship with Jesus— even as one mystical body with him.

This intimate relationship is described by the author of John with the image, rooted in Psalm 80, of the vine and the branches, where the disciple is nourished by the love of Jesus. Those who abide in his love will bear fruit (15:1-11), manifest in one's love for others. This love in Jesus is most deeply expressed within the community, where the disciples are to love one another in joy. Apart from Jesus the community can do nothing; quite literally, the disciple has life through a personal, mystical union with Jesus. Thus this unnamed disciple on the shore of Tiberias is perhaps more deeply injured and more alone than any of the others. He lost a loved one, a partner, a parent. His isolation is that of the bereaved, the one who goes searching for the departed in everything he does. His grief is that of his community as well, for in losing Jesus it loses the very purpose of its existence.

Why are they all here? It is an odd group assembled on the shore—odd because these are not all fishermen and odd in the way they are identified. John has previously referred to the followers of Jesus as "the disciples," those who share in the intimate relationship of vine and branch, but here he is careful to name all but two of them. Of the "other two disciples of his," one is the "disciple whom Jesus loved." But who is the other? Likely candidates include Andrew and Philip, who are otherwise prominent in John, and Mary Magdalene, the first to visit the tomb and the first to see the risen Lord. Mary is especially appealing to me as the unknown other on the shore. She is the first to the tomb in John 20. She runs immediately to Simon Peter and to "the other disciple, the one whom Jesus loved," to tell them the news that the stone has been removed. She remains behind in the garden after the two disciples return to their homes—and she is the first to see the risen Jesus, reporting her encounter to the others. But in Chapter 21, there is a recollection of only two previous sightings of the risen Jesus. Mary's meeting with the Lord seems to have been forgotten or suppressed. Nor is her having been the first to see him honored in the community's memory. So her unnamed presence here would stand as a reminder of what has been removed from the official story: that voice of the "other," the one who speaks only for her own experience, the truthful witness.

As they look around at each other, these people—remnants of a community devastated by loss—might be struck by their individual and collective failings. Peter has pulled his boat onto the sand and they get in. James and John are folding the net in place. There is nothing for the others to do because they know nothing about fishing. Each of the named witnesses has in some way misunderstood, denied, or challenged Jesus—Peter most vividly in the courtyard. James and John wanted preferment. Thomas wanted proof. Nathanael wanted a better class of messiah. Each of them seems to be in need of reconciliation. They enter the boat in isolation from one another and from their own story, which has brought them to this place. Do they trust Peter to take them to where the fish are? Wariness settles over a boat suddenly filled with strangers.

The condition of isolation in which we find these disciples is at the heart of our sense of ourselves when we are separated from God. God is revealed most fully in relatedness; that is what the Resurrection affirms. Death outside of community is the isolation that Peter knows—and that so many of us know. This isolation is something we all feel on occasion in our lives. As I am using the word here, isolation is a negative condition. It is not solitude or a creative retreat. It is not St. John of the Cross's "dark night of the soul." It is what Kierkegaard called "the sickness until death"—quite simply, despair. As he describes this condition, it is a sickness that has no apparent hope, not even the hope of release through death. It is a condition without God.

The disciples did not know who they were any more. The supports had been taken away from them. It

happens to all of us at different times in our lives. A
divorce, the loss of a job, the death of a loved one—any
such event can suddenly make us doubt that there was
ever anyone other than ourselves. We imagine ourselves
to be profoundly alone. It is in this condition that we
most often are found by God, who, as we read in Exodus 2:24, hears the cries of the people and, remembering the covenant, comes to them. First we have to cry
out, however. We have to initiate the search for God.

Six years ago, I lost my job as director of a publishing company, and afterwards I felt completely lost. I
asked myself, "Now that I do not have this job, who
am I?" I fell into a state of helplessness and hopeless-
ness that was compounded by the fact that my marriage
of eighteen years was over and that I had moved into
a tiny rented room. At the age of forty-nine, everything
that I had taken for granted about myself was being
called into question. On the index of stressful life
events, I experienced three of the worst all at once.

Not long after my job ended, I flew to Costa Rica
to fish for rainbow bass on Lake Arenal. It was in many
ways a perfect sign of my emotional and spiritual state.
The lake is located in a part of the country that was
reachable over an unpaved road that traversed a bleak,
sparsely populated landscape. I was staying in the town
of La Fortuna—a nice irony, I thought—at the eastern
end of the lake in the shadow of an active volcano. The
evening before I was to meet my guide for the day's
fishing I accompanied a tourist group to the slopes of
the volcano to watch it spit fire into the night. The air
smelled of sulphur. Beneath our feet the volcano rum-
bled. Above us it belched smoke and fiery ashes. Was
there any chance of escape, someone asked, if Arenal

erupted right now? There was none, our guide told us with a flash of teeth in the dark.

The next morning I met my guide before dawn. He was a native who spoke virtually no English and my Spanish was primitive. On the shore, I could sense the volcano behind me. It was hidden in the rising morning mists, as was the lake and the shore across the water. From where I stood, I had no sense of place or direction. Fortunately, I had a guide who knew what he was doing. All I had to do was listen to him, go where he said to go, cast where he pointed. Good fishing guides will help an angler catch fish. They do it in subtle ways, positioning you to put your fly where the fish are. The guide knows their habits, how they behave at different times of the day or in different weather. We prowled an area at the end of the lake under the volcano, the top of which remained shrouded in cloud through the morning. The shore was a lava field. Beneath the surface of the water I could see stumps of old trees, charred stalks.

My guide knew the water. He took me to the fish, but I was too quick each time a fish struck at my fly. I yanked it in anticipation of the expected hit and, in effect, pulled the hook away before the fish could bite. My guide worked on me to be more patient. I was not in the mood to be patient. I wanted a big rainbow bass and a photograph that would show how good, how powerful, I was. And so I caught nothing. By the time the sun was well up in the sky, the good morning fishing time was over. We went ashore to eat eggs and beans-and-rice with strong coffee in a small thatched hut by the lake. I wanted to go back and try again. But the guide told me to rest awhile. The fish were going to cooler depths. We would go back shortly and try again.

Although I hooked two fish before the day was over, both of which dove to the bottom and wrapped my line around the stumps to break it, I did not land any bass that day. It was my birthday. I was fifty years old and unemployed and wondered, as I drove back along the lake toward San José, what was to become of me.

The isolation I felt in La Fortuna, under the volcano, and on the fishing boat was deep. What should have been a joyous adventure was disappointing and ultimately sad. It was not that I caught no fish, but that I did not understand where or who I was. You cannot catch fish if you do not know the territory you inhabit and if you lack confidence in yourself. I was a stranger and felt like a stranger, even to myself. I wanted epiphany as well as fish. I got neither.

In a sense, I was that other, unnamed disciple on the shore of Lake Tiberias and in the boat on that fishless night. Anyone could be that mysterious other, including you and me, and perhaps that is as good a solution to the question of identity as any. It is easy to put ourselves into that place, that frame of mind, and remember what it is like to be lost, to be broken, to be in jeopardy. Each of us has been here, on this bleak shore, under a volcano, uncertain about whom to follow or what to do next. It is perhaps as close to a universal human experience as one can describe.

 Isolation is a spiritual condition because it is a place of separation from the life of the spirit. It is a condition that most of us immediately recognize. I have been there. I have been in a room crowded with people that I do not know, all of them ignoring me. I have been in a town in which no one spoke my language when I needed help. I have been locked up, either physically or emotionally, because of my self-

destructive actions. Sometimes we get stuck in this
dimension for long periods of time. We climb out of
it and then fall back in. Our expectations become dis-
appointed. We go to work at a job that we hate but
cannot escape, or we enter into a relationship that is
damaging to our sense of self or injures us physically.
We make mistakes and come to believe that there is
no way to remedy them. We abandon the ones we
love, or they abandon us.

I have been in these states many times in my life. I
have thought that my errors, my mistakes in judgment,
had finished me—as I did for a long time after losing
my job at the university. It seemed that there was no
redemption for me. There was nothing I could do. In
effect, this is a dimension of no faith at all in which we
feel that we alone are responsible for making things
happen in our lives. It is also a state of mind in which
we frequently feel that God is the Punitive Other—the
Judge out there who no longer has any patience with
us. Many of us have carried—and still carry—these
primitive notions of God as the demanding overseer,
not a loving shepherd, not the father welcoming home
the prodigal. These images come out of our child-
hood, rooted in those stories in the Hebrew scriptures
of the wrathful God who slaughters the enemies of
Israel. The twelve-year-old believer continues to
inhabit our heads and, in times of trouble, takes charge.
This kid has nowhere to turn when God runs into the
bedroom in the middle of the night swinging a belt.
The image of a child quavering under the bed is not
one that inspires adult hope.

The disciples push off from the shore in Peter's
boat, aware of their errors and uncertainties. They

cannot see where they are going. They proceed by faith—or is it reckless abandon? This boat is filled with amateurs. The lake can be stormy. James and John are on the oars. Peter is looking gloomily into the dark. The unnamed disciples are napping in the bow. Thomas is on the rudder. Nathanael would be reading a book if it were daylight and if books existed.

It is easy to think of the boat as an image of the fragile early church—or of the church at any time. In it, we have to depend on each other and on our individual abilities. If we are in the boat together, and working in concert, we will more likely reach the shore, catch our fish, or weather the storm. Stories abound in the gospels of the disciples being together in the boat. Jesus usually is with them or comes to them to make their passage easier, safer, or more reliable. They never catch fish without him. The boat can also be a kind of prison—surrounded by water, or caught in a storm, with no place to go and no one else to turn to. This is also a reason why people are wary of close community: if I throw in my lot with you and you turn out to be unreliable or less than I need, what am I to do? Look at all of the time I will waste. I may lose money or prestige. If you do not know how to handle a boat, I may also lose my life.

Peter's boat is not yet a church. It is not a community. Its inhabitants lack the maturity that breaks through the shell of individual anxieties and fears, while true community requires significant effort and, usually, the sacrifice of our personal agendas. It requires giving up some piece of ourselves. What kills community faster than anything else is the insistence on being right. If I cannot meet you where you are, and understand what you are feeling—if my only goal is to convince you that my position is right and yours is wrong—then we will not achieve community.

A key to breaking out of our isolation may be to appreciate the difference between thinking alike and feeling alike. It is rare for two or more people actually to think alike—to share not only opinions but to agree on the way in which something should be done. The Myers-Briggs Test, which is so popular among church people, helps to demonstrate how different we are in our ways of thinking and of processing information. Knowing how people think can help us get along with one another. If I know your personality type, at least I can thxen understand why you do not get what I am saying and I can change the way I present my ideas so that you will hear them better. But that may not be enough to bring us to a place in which we can do something useful together. I may understand how you think and still be unable to be in community with you.

If I understand that you have feelings that are like mine—if I know that you are as threatened as I am by being contradicted or proved wrong—then I can appreciate your reaction when I disagree with you. I can remind myself that you are afraid of losing face or of having to admit that you made an error. You may be embarrassed. You may need emotional support. I am like you in all of those ways. If we can separate the fact that we do not think alike from the emotional needs we share, then we might be able to find some common ground in our humanity on which to be together. We can be in relationship. Does it help to know that someone who molests young children also has fears? Yes, it does, even though that would not lead me to entrust that person with my young children. Although I still may not be able to be in intimate community with such a person, he or she should not be beyond the circle of our community's concern or caring. No one is disposable in the beloved community.

Alone on the boat at night the disciples were undoubtedly experiencing similar emotions: fear, uncertainty, anxiety about the future, frustration, anger with each other, ordinary unhappiness, loneliness. That they were all in one boat did not prevent their feeling these emotions, even all of them. They felt cut off from God in some significant ways, it seems. The ocean or deep water is a place for meeting God. Catching fish is usually a sign of God's bounty. Not catching fish is a sign of God's absence. If there are no fish in the water, it is like being in the desert where nothing lives. If we cast our nets repeatedly and catch nothing, we begin to feel abandoned by life itself. I have felt this on streams and in the ocean, days and nights when it seemed clear that there was no longer life in the water. The emptiness grows until everything is swallowed up in it. Like a night sky in which there are no stars, the blackness denies all presence. When one is on the ocean under a starless sky, the sense of being anywhere at all disappears. The person who is sitting in the boat or standing in the water disappears.

There are spiritual conditions in which such encounters with emptiness are filled with the divine, but when we are isolated from ourselves and from God, when we assume that we alone are responsible for making the universe accountable, then we can find in such emptiness only absence. The more we insist on being heard, the more silent and dark the night becomes. The absence of God is the absence of community. It is the absence of others. On the boat on the Sea of Tiberias, these disciples are together but profoundly apart, each

Keep on trying.

Perfect moment

in his own world of uneasiness or even guilt. They have gone fishing in a state of mind in which catching fish is virtually impossible because they are focused almost entirely on their own concerns, their own needs.

When I am at peace with myself, at home in the natural world—when I am in a state of relatedness to myself and creation—I catch fish. It is that simple and that certain. I feel what is happening in the water and can tell where the fish are and what they might be eating. The first time I understood what it meant to feel this aliveness in water I was on the Octoraro Creek in central Pennsylvania. It was a warm summer day. I stood in the cool flow of the water trying to decide what artificial fly to choose. Then I recalled seeing grasshoppers in the grass by the creek—and at the same time *knew* that there was a trout across from me, near the opposite bank. The fish was behind a dead branch angled into the water. I also saw, in my mind, a grasshopper falling off the branch into the waiting mouth of the fish. I tied an artificial grasshopper onto my fly line, flicked the line back and forth over my head until I had unrolled thirty feet of monofilament, and dropped the hopper on the branch. It sat there a moment and then slipped off into the stream. Instantly, the fish I knew had to be there splashily took the fly. It was a perfect moment.

This state of connectedness does not happen very often. When it does, I feel suddenly as if the boundaries of my being have been opened and what is out there mixes freely with what is inside myself. It is as if my body were covered with tastebuds, as the scales of fish are, and I could indeed taste everything around me—as if I were immersed wholly in the tastiness of all that is. When I heard that fish have tastebuds on

me

in confirmation class, w a fellow student - connected in nature their scales, I understood for the first time what it might mean to "taste and see that the Lord is good."

We cannot taste everything, or even anything, if we are hermetically sealed, if we block ourselves from the cares and joys of others. The community into which Jesus summoned his disciples was one in which each might be the celebrant of God's goodness for the others. Such community is difficult to create, as these Christians who struggled to form the church discovered. How were they to reconcile their differing visions of what Jesus had called them to do? The problem must have seemed insurmountable. The question of who is enabled to interpret the teachings of Jesus has been central to the life of the church. It was profound for John's community as the church was emerging at the end of the first century, and it should be equally profound for us at the beginning of the third millennium, when many churches are facing a crisis of survival.

The problem facing the disciples on the lake during that long night of catching no fish was that they were not in community with one another and did not know how to get there. They were isolated both from each other and from a clear understanding of what they were called to do or who they were called, as individuals or a community, to be. It is the condition of churches today, and it is deadly for the future of a Christianity that is open to growth and freedom, a Christianity that does not demand conformity or the loss of individual creativity, a Christianity that is not founded on dogma but on the living presence of the Christ, who leads not to law but to wisdom.

Peter exemplifies the isolate who, like so many of us, gets up every day and goes to work. He looks out at the sea and thinks the fish might be biting. Time to get on with life. But he is not getting on with life. He is simply going to work. He has no understanding of vocation, what Jesus has called him to be. He is not aware that he has already died to the old life of fisherman. Because he has not been reborn to a new understanding of life, he has no hope and no way to be with God. That is why there are no fish. What he is trying to do does not match who he is called to be.

How does Peter—or how do any of us—escape this condition of isolation, this place of despair, and discover life in the waters? The treatment for Peter's sickness and for ours is precisely to be found in death and resurrection. Which is why Jesus reveals himself in and through them.

Chapter 2

"It Is the Lord!"

4 Just after daybreak, Jesus stood on the beach; but the disciples did not know that it was Jesus. 5 Jesus said to them, "Children, you have no fish, have you?" They answered him, "No." 6 He said to them, "Cast the net to the right side of the boat, and you will find some." So they cast it, and now they were not able to haul it in because there were so many fish. 7 That disciple whom Jesus loved said to Peter, "It is the Lord!" When Simon Peter heard that it was the Lord, he put on some clothes, for he was naked, and jumped into the sea. 8 But the other disciples came in the boat, dragging the net full of fish, for they were not far from the land, only about a hundred yards off.

After daybreak, when the disciples have been fishing all night and have caught nothing, Jesus appears on the shore. But at first they do not recognize him. Why should they? It has been a long night, and Jesus is dead. It could be anybody. At this time of the morning, there is undoubtedly a haze on the water. The air is almost blue. Nothing is as it seems. The disciples in the boat have to be tired. Those who have been working the nets feel it in their arms and backs, especially since this is an activity they have not pursued in three or four years. Once toughened hands are scraped and perhaps even bleeding. What about the others? Have they been napping? Quarreling? Reminiscing? All we know from this story is that someone from the beach calls out to the boat, "Children, you have no fish, have you?" It could be almost mocking in tone. If there are other fishing boats nearby, perhaps the fishermen in them laugh at the question. The disciples might be annoyed that the stranger has called attention to their empty nets. Peter, James, and John once made their living at this and now they are singled out as amateurs.

Worse yet, the stranger has the audacity to tell them where to put their nets when they, not he, have been out working these waters all night. There are clearly no fish here. When they cast their nets to the right side of the boat, Peter surely does it in anger, with perhaps a "watch this if you're so smart" look at the man who stands smugly on dry land. But immediately the nets are filled. They begin to teem with unexpected life. The surface of the water is roiling with fish. Even the napping disciples sit up and take notice. Among them is the Beloved Disciple, who perhaps has been listening to the exchange between Peter and the stranger with amusement. He likes it when Peter is taken down a peg or two. The big fisherman who never listens to anyone takes instruction from a nobody on the beach.

But when the nets are filled, the Beloved Disciple suddenly understands what has happened. He hears that voice calling from the shore in a new way. He recognizes it. This is the voice that makes things happen, the one who changes reality, repairs what is broken, creates life. The Beloved Disciple says to Peter, "It is the Lord!" Incredibly, he knows that the stranger is Jesus. Hearing this news, Peter plunges without hesitating into the sea and swims toward the one who had been crucified. The others follow in the lumbering boat, dragging their catch to the shore. All of them still waking up.

The disciples have not been looking for Jesus as he was but have been searching for something that disappeared when he died. Because they have not been able to articulate what they need, they do not at first recognize what they are looking at. The presence of the Lord is revealed to them, as it always is, unexpectedly and mysteriously. Not without being in some way summoned, however: in going out in the boat to fish, this band of seekers has been engaged in a form of prayer. The dark night, as St. John of the Cross wrote, "with its aridities and voids is the means to the knowledge of God and self."[1]

Biblical stories like this one can be seen as accounts of seeking God's will, finding it out for ourselves. The model for this search is the story of the people of Israel whose wanderings in the Sinai were just such a discerning of the spirits. Soon after crossing the Sea of Reeds, and after traveling for three days without water in the wilderness of Shur, the Israelites came to Marah, where the water was bitter. They complained to Moses, who sweetened the water with a piece of wood. Then the Lord said: "If you will listen carefully to the voice of the Lord your God, and do what is right in his sight, . . . I will not bring upon you any of the diseases that I brought upon the Egyptians; for I am the Lord who heals you" (Ex. 15:22–26). They then entered the wilderness of Sin, where again they complained against

---

1. St. John of the Cross, "The Dark Night," in Kieran Kavanaugh OCD, and Otilio Rodriguez OCD, trans., *The Collected Works of St. John of the Cross* (Washington, DC: ICS Publications, 1979), p. 323.

Moses because they were hungry. The Lord tells Moses that he will send bread from heaven, which is to be gathered each day for that day only. "In the evening you shall know that it was the Lord who brought you out of the land of Egypt, and in the morning you shall see the glory of the Lord" (Ex. 16:1–7). This phrase, the "glory"of the Lord, appears here for the first time in Scripture; God's essential nature is revealed in providing for his people's needs.[2] This presence is what the disciples sought, and what we seek as well.

This time in the wilderness without water means, according to one interpretation, that God had not bestowed on the people any new revelation. They experienced no renewal, even though they had been liberated from slavery. They found no desire or delight.[3] It was, in other words, a time of boredom, a time of waiting for something to happen. In emptiness, they saw only emptiness and none of the possibilities that emptiness might hold. They desired nothing meaningful, only to be given food and drink. Wilderness is empty space, and one might plausibly describe the time spent by the people of Israel in this empty space as one of looking not for a way out, but for a purpose, a reason for being a people at all. They were discerning who they were in order to understand better where they were going. Their forty-years' journey to the Promised Land is the definitive proof that the course of meaning never does run smoothly. We seldom see where we are going when the Spirit tells us to get up and go. And God seldom makes the highway straight for us.

2. My discussion here owes a lot to Avivah Gottleib Zornberg's book, *The Particulars of Rapture: Reflections on Exodus* (New York: Doubleday, 2001), especially Chapter 4, pp. 231-36.
3. Tanchuma Beshallach, 24, in Zornberg, p. 233

The disciples in their fishing boat are also like the
people of Israel in the desert after their escape from
Egypt. The Sea of Tiberias at night when the fish are
not biting is a wilderness too. One way to describe
wilderness is "trackless waste." There are no apparent
signs to lead one to familiar territory, and so we wander aimlessly. The fish do not bite when we do not
understand the water, when we do not recognize the
landscape. We drift from place to place and hope for
the best. The long night drifting in the boat is boring.
The water appears to be empty of all life—although in
fact it is not. Wilderness, it turns out, is in the eye of
the beholder. Your trackless waste is my backyard. The
disciples who have lost their master and their way cannot come up with any reason for being. Where the
people of Israel sought water for their thirst, the disciples seek fish without knowing why. Both search
blindly in the midst of abundance for abundance.
The Presence is everywhere. The task is to see it.

Discernment is the 2nd dimension of Spiritual Maturity

The second dimension of spiritual maturity is discernment, a term I first encountered in the early eight-
ies, soon after I was confirmed in the Episcopal
Church, following sixteen years of separation from any
formal church tradition. The rector of my parish in
Philadelphia followed the Ignatian form of discerning
the spirits practiced by Jesuits, which involves entering into biblical stories as a way of sorting out God's
will for our lives. He invited me to join him in this
process of discernment for my own life.

One midnight I was in my third-floor study reflecting on Moses and the burning bush, as I had been asked
to do, when I heard a crash in the street. I looked out
the window and saw a car burst into flame. How was

I to relate this odd experience to God's will for my life? Later I came to understand that while I might be seeking a message (and in a couple of instances Jesus seemed to speak to me directly) what I generally experienced was an outward sign of my internal spiritual state. This discerning of spirits was a way of understanding more fully the state of my relatedness to God. These were signs that helped to point me in the right direction.

Knowing who we are helps us to understand where we are going. Spiritual practice—regularly engaging in prayer and meditation, corporate worship, the study of Scripture—keeps us fit, as it were, for the times when we doubt who we are and whether we are going anywhere at all. Those first efforts at discernment, known as spiritual exercises, taught me the value of doing the soul's work, even when the results were hard to understand. They also taught me to do that work with others. The way out of our isolation is through spiritual practice in community: discerning the spirits in our life journeys. The disciples in their dark night come to the knowledge of God and self through a deeper awareness of life with others.

When something new comes into our lives, we are compelled to look in a different direction. How we determine whether God is calling us—or whether we are simply distracted—is the difficulty. *Why* is that car burning in the street just as I am reading about Moses and the burning bush? There may be no meaning to the coincidence at all. The important questions are: What does the experience tell us to do? What does it give us? Jesus gives the disciples explicit instructions—cast the nets to the right side of the boat. When the disciples do as they are told, they haul in a net full of

fish. Something happens. The Beloved Disciple then
realizes that it is the Lord who has called to them
because he recognizes the One who brings abundance.
His understanding is awakened by what he knows. This
event is not unusual at all. It is characteristic of Jesus.
Our reactions can be different when we understand
that God is calling us—Peter acts, John is more contemplative. Peter makes the precipitous move toward
commitment, plunging into the sea. He goes to the
beckoning Christ. He has acted impetuously before,
not always with good results. The Beloved Disciple
brings everyone else with him.

In this second dimension of our journey toward wisdom, this time of discernment, we learn to pay attention to the signs in our lives, especially in our dark
nights, that lead us to a better understanding of God's
will. How do we do that? How do I know that God is
speaking to me? One clue is supplied in this passage:
"That disciple whom Jesus loved said to Peter, 'It is the
Lord!'" Thus, the identity of the one on the shore is
confirmed by the church, which is a community of
interpretation. Another clue is, as I have already said,
that the result of hearing and acting on God's word is
abundance—in this case, a huge catch of fish.

Discernment is not possible in isolation—at least, I
do not think it is. We need at least one other, such as
a spiritual friend, but preferably a community, to help
us sort out the options before us. It is one of the reasons, I think, that the church is an assembly. It is the
place in which Jesus rises to new life. Yet how do we
form community when we are in a state of isolation? It
is the question facing us in virtually every aspect of
contemporary life, including the church, in which our
individualistic theology can work against spiritual

growth and maturity. A theology that mystifies Jesus, that diminishes his humanity, can also be an impediment to intimate community, especially if we depend on the magic of the sacrament to manage spiritual crisis.

Peter, as well as the Beloved Disciple and the others in this boat (which we might also call the church), are not without resources. They have been with Jesus and have learned more than they know. All of us are more capable than we realize. We are better than we think. We are stronger than the internal voices that regularly tell us how deeply we have failed. Even though the disciples—and these disciples in particular—have betrayed Jesus and his vision of community, they nonetheless were with him in his ministry and came to know at some deep level what they were being asked to do and who they were called to be. The power of the church is awakened from a deep contemplative sleep by the risen Jesus who, as he does in this story, calls out to the sleepers.

When Jesus calls from the shore, it seems to me it is almost like being called in a dream. Can't you hear this in a dream? "Children, you have no fish, have you?" And the disciples point to the empty nets: Hello? No fish! Then, the nets are full of the fish that were there all along. This experience has the advantage of being a common one for anglers. I remember once fishing in a trout stream in Pennsylvania, catching nothing and being puzzled about the empty waters, when I looked behind me and saw, lined up in the protection of my legs, several trout happily feeding. There was no way to drop a fly back there, and they seemed to know it.

A dream will often incorporate sounds from the sleeper's environment or be changed by the presence of someone else by the bed. It often happens that something in the world invades our dream and wakes us. The reality enters the dream and calls us back. In fact, the disciples do wake up, which is the classic description of what happens when we encounter the divine. We awaken to reality. What wakes these hapless fishermen is the abundance and generosity that reminds them of the experience of God in Jesus. That, and the voice of the divine, which we can recognize even in our sleep. This voice often comes from the mouth of someone we know and trust. For the disciples, this voice belongs to Jesus, the one they knew intimately.

God's abundance does not lead necessarily to personal glory or wealth, as James and John expected, or the vindication of one's point of view, as Peter often hoped. Nor does it settle any argument, as Thomas hoped when he touched the risen Lord. In abundance, we recognize God's essential nature. And it is the opposite of isolation. It is also more generous, more welcoming than we thought.

In the church, as in our lives, we need to be in a constant state of discernment, testing what comes to us, questioning what is in us. We are not seeking what is out there so much as what is in here. Therefore, at the heart of this state is spiritual practice: regular prayer and time alone with ourselves in God. Without that kind of practice, we cannot hear what our community is saying (nor can we speak effectively in it), and we cannot recognize what increases God's abundance for others. So we need both private time and community time.

The kind of spiritual practice I am talking about here is deeper than a regular reading of Scripture or saying morning and evening prayer, or even a daily presence at the Eucharist. These are important Christian disciplines, of course, but they are all oriented toward the spoken word. That is one of the characteristics of Christian worship, of course, that we hear and speak the word in order to understand what God requires of us. Corporate worship in the Protestant tradition is focused on preaching; in some denominations the Eucharist has become more central, but there is still a lot of talk. Finding moments of silence in church is a challenge, and I have discovered that introducing silence is disconcerting for most worshipers. Even a pause of ten seconds can throw people into a state of uneasiness. Papers begin to rustle. Feet tap the floor. People check their watches. At a church I recently served, I introduced the Taizé style of worship as a midweek option and found that no one was able to sustain a silence of longer than five minutes and even that was more than most really wanted.

Since we call Jesus the Word of God, it is perhaps not surprising that our religion is intensely verbal. Being with Scripture, listening to spoken prayers, and feeling the power of the sung consecration of bread and wine can all be richly enlivening. But at the same time it can block our deeper understanding of what it is God might be saying to us or asking of us. The spiritual practice I am talking about here is rooted in two spiritual attitudes or conditions that are not at all about speaking or even hearing speech. They prepare us to hear, however, both what our community might be saying and what God is saying.

Both of the attitudes I want to focus on are represented by Peter and the Beloved Disciple in this scene in the fishing boat. One is listening and the other is nakedness. The Beloved Disciple is the only one who recognizes the voice of Jesus. As an intimate, one who lies at the teacher's breast, he has been listening. He is the quiet one—often present but seldom heard. We feel his presence in the Gospel of John, whereas we hear Peter and see him in action. But Peter represents the other side of the attitude of listening and that is of nakedness. In the boat, he is naked. He is also naked in his responses throughout John—quick to reply or act, often without thinking. The author of John seems to portray this characteristic of Peter negatively, as suggested by his pairing Peter with Judas. He also indicates by the attention he pays to Peter and the Beloved Disciple throughout the gospel that the two of them are essential in some way to the life of the church.

We need to listen for something other than words, for what is behind or beyond language, and we need to be naked in the presence of God and in the presence of others. Both attitudes seem to be contrary to all of our basic instincts for self-preservation. When we listen carefully, we have to give up for the time being our own assumptions and to suppress our need to be heard. We also associate nakedness with shame, with exposure, with discomfort, except in the most intimate environments. In most of our human encounters, we are unable or unwilling to say what we actually think. We restrict what we say for a lot of reasons, often because we do not believe that what we really think will be welcome in given circumstances. This is the case even among members of our families with whom, in fact, we often monitor ourselves most severely. These two conditions go together. If we are censoring our thoughts, we are not listening. If we are protecting our nakedness, we are not available to the intimate community that abides in God's love.

The Beloved Disciple is described as being closest to Jesus. He is not referred to by name but as the "one whom Jesus loved." That is who he is. He is the one whose connection with Jesus is at the heart of the spirituality of John's community. This spirituality is most explicitly described in John 15, where Jesus speaks of himself as the true vine and those who abide in his love as the branches and commands the disciples to love one another. "As the Father has loved me, so I have loved you; abide in my love. . . .This is my commandment, that you love one another as I have loved you" (John 15:9, 12). To abide in this love is to be nourished in all ways, nurtured in body and soul, so that, like the vine, we grow abundantly. It is to abide in an attitude of complete attention, always listening or watching. What we are listening or watching for are the signs of God's presence—not words, not even meaning.

I once did a spiritual exercise that included a meditation on this passage from John. Next to my house in Philadelphia at the time was an abandoned house. From our grape-vine trellis in the backyard, the vines had climbed over the fence along the telephone and electric lines into the abandoned house. The leaves emerged from various broken windows, rioting it seemed in the pleasure of simply growing. The empty house came alive with the vines, and I thought that that exuberance was an important image of oneness with God. When I met with my spiritual director, however, he suggested that I meditate on the need for pruning in healthy vineyards. He was referring to that part of John 15 that speaks of God as the vine-grower who

removes the barren branches that do not bear fruit—
and prunes those that do bear fruit so that they can bear
even more. "The time of pruning is beloved," he told
me. I liked the sound of that without knowing what it
felt like to be pruned. I assumed that I was the one with
the shears. Later, when I was seriously pruned following the loss of my job, I thought about that image and
found that I did not love the time of pruning at all. I
hated it. What I did understand was that I could not
bear fruit by myself but needed the presence of others
and the presence of God in them. Discerning the sense
of that sign has been an elaborated process of listening, which I have only come to appreciate in writing
about it here years later.

The character of John's community suggested by
these images of the vineyard is one of intimate relatedness that requires careful listening, and it is personified in the Beloved Disciple. Our ears need to be
tuned, as another passage says, to the voice of the shepherd. So when Jesus reveals the abundance of creation
through a huge catch of tilapia and sardines (big ones),
the Beloved Disciple recognizes his voice: "It is the
Lord!" This recognition wakes them up. Their illusion
of being isolated and abandoned disappears instantly.
For the first time they see where they are and who they
are and what they are capable of doing. Jesus does not
do this for them. They have been out there fishing all
night, working at it. They have not forgotten the skills
they once had.

This moment of recognition is a recollection of
intimacy. Listening is a healing act. A personal God is
one who can be known intimately: being in the presence of someone who knows us well is healing. To be
known, to be understood, is the basic human need at

the center of our intimate relations with others. Prayer opens us to God so that we can be known, and in being known, come to know ourselves. The prayer of attention is at the heart of intimacy with God, as indeed attentiveness is at the heart of our intimacy with each other. In contemplative prayer we come into God's presence without language, expecting no words of welcome or appreciation. We simply allow ourselves to be still and to be. This practice is hard for us because our minds are always filled with snatches of memory, words, songs, experiences, pictures, anxieties. Try to sit still without thinking of anything. It is difficult, if not impossible. We expect to be filled. We fear being empty—and complete silence, even silence in our heads—feels like emptiness and therefore seems meaningless. The opposite is true. Clearing our minds of the memories, words, songs, experiences, pictures, and anxieties that impede God allows the presence to be with us.

But what are we listening for, if not language? For each of us, the answer is different. We may indeed hear something like words, as in this story from John 21 the Beloved Disciple hears Jesus. But he hears more than just Jesus. He hears a resonance like the plucked string of a violin in his very being. He does not say, "It is Jesus." He says, "It is the Lord." In my experience on the Hudson River, which I describe in the Introduction to this book, I "heard" the Lord in my vision of the boat on the river. I heard more than the words of the Scripture I had been reading. I heard more than mere meaning. In fact, what I describe as a call to ministry in the vision of a boat might be a sign of mental illness in some people, but for me the boat was a vehicle to sanity.

When the prophet Elijah fled to the wilderness to die, he ended up on Horeb, the mountain of God. There, the word of the Lord came to him, asking, "What are you doing here, Elijah?" The Lord asked him to stand on the mountain, "for the Lord is about to pass by."

> Now there was a great wind, so strong that it was split-ting mountains and breaking rocks in pieces before the Lord, but the Lord was not in the wind; and after the wind an earthquake, but the Lord was not in the earth-quake; and after the earthquake a fire, but the Lord was not in the fire; and after the fire a sound of sheer silence. When Elijah heard it, he wrapped his face in his mantle and went out and stood at the entrance of the cave (1 Kings 19:9–13).

What Elijah "heard" in the silence opens him up to the word of the Lord for his life. That is what we are lis-tening for, however it is given. For the disciples in the fishing boat, the word was the Resurrected One who stood on the shore. It was not what he said but who he was for them that called them into their future.

Nakedness in Scripture almost always means shame, judgment, or obligation. To be naked is to be a sign of offense to society or God, an indication of unworthiness. Out of religious duty, the righteous are to clothe the naked who lack clothing through no fault of their own. But there is another category of nakedness that is an image of spiritual openness to God. This nakedness implies worth. Because it is very rare in the Bible, it is all the more noteworthy. When Peter, of all people, gets naked, we have to pay attention.

"When Simon Peter heard that it was the Lord, he put on some clothes, for he was naked, and jumped into the sea." Peter responds to events honestly and, often, impulsively. His instincts and energy take over. This passage (as it appears in the NRSV) says that he is literally naked (although other translations suggest that he is naked under some other garment). Commentators fall all over themselves trying to figure this out. Was he really naked? How could that be? Why would the author of John 21 refer to Peter's nakedness at all? They offer explanations that explain nothing except their own uneasiness with this oddity. I would like to stay with the image of the naked Peter, out there in the boat with no protection from the elements. He is completely vulnerable. When the call comes from Jesus, there is nothing between him and the one who helps him to see his true self. At the same time he is completely exposed. It is so different from his behavior in the hours before Jesus was crucified, when Peter hid himself in denial and fear.

Peter's nakedness can be better understood, I think, in light of those few other passages in Scripture where nakedness invites divine presence into the human heart. Together with listening, this nakedness is the spiritual practice so necessary for discernment.

The original couple, Adam and Eve, "were both naked, and were not ashamed" (Gen. 2:25) until they had separated themselves from God. Then, suddenly they "knew that they were naked" (Gen. 3:7) and clothed themselves out of a new-found shame. They were no longer intimate with God—and with each other felt new uneasiness. Another form of spiritual nakedness is prophetic, in which being naked is part of a statement of God's favor toward the one who dares to take off clothes in the presence of the divine. Saul fell "into a prophetic frenzy . . . stripped off his clothes . . . [and] lay naked all that day and all that night" (1 Sam. 19:23–24). Likewise, Isaiah was sent by God to walk "naked and barefoot for three years as a sign and a portent against Egypt and Ethiopia" (Isa. 20:3). In 2 Samuel, King David "danced before the Lord with all his might; David was girded with a linen ephod," a hip-length garment under which David seems to have been naked. His dancing must have revealed his nakedness, for his wife Michal criticizes him for "uncovering himself." David defends himself by saying, "It was before the Lord" (2 Sam. 6:14, 20–21). His nakedness is part of a ritual in which he is both priest and king, a rite of passage in which ordinary human dignity is less important than the act of honoring the Lord.

Most provocative perhaps is that strange moment in Mark's Gospel during Jesus' arrest: "A certain young man was following him, wearing nothing but a linen cloth. They [the soldiers] caught hold of him, but he left the linen cloth and ran off naked" (Mk. 14:51–52). The noncanonical Secret Gospel of Mark identifies this young man with Lazarus and dramatically describes Jesus' rolling away the stone from the entrance to the tomb and raising him up. The young man "looked at Jesus, loved him, and began to beg him to be with him." Six days later, Jesus called the young man, "a linen cloth having been draped over the naked body," to him. "He spent the night with him, because Jesus taught him the mystery of God's domain" (Secret Mark 1:1–13). This same young man appears at the empty tomb and announces to the women who come to the tomb that Jesus has risen.

This naked young man is probably a student (a catechuman), and his nakedness is a sign either of his innocence or ignorance. He has not yet been initiated into the mysteries. His presence suggests the catechumans in the early church who were baptized naked by equally naked presbyters; it is likely that this tantalizing text refers to the period of time in which those desiring entry into the church were taught the doctrines of the faith. Then, stripped for baptism, they meet the risen Lord as they themselves, having been buried with Christ in his death, are raised to new life with him.

Peter's leap into the sea sounds a lot like baptism. He throws a garment over his nakedness, but it is no more effective or important than the ephod David wore when he danced in the streets of Jerusalem. The garment Peter wears is more like a liturgical drape that signifies his swim to Jesus as a rite of passage. It also recalls that moment in John's Gospel when Jesus washes the disciples' feet in John 13. When Jesus has taken off his outer robe (undressed, in effect, although it is not suggested that he is naked), he begins to wash feet and wipe them dry. Peter objects, "You will never wash my feet." Jesus replies, "Unless I wash you, you have no share with me." And Peter exclaims, "Lord, not my feet only but also my hands and my head!" (Jn. 13:4–9). Now, Peter leaps into the sea as into baptism, to be washed clean of whatever has kept him from understanding what he has been called to do as one who followed Jesus when he was alive. He plunges in and swims toward the Lord, leaving his isolation behind.

The naked hear God's voice. That is one way to describe what I have been teasing out of this experience the disciples have of being called from isolation into community by the risen Christ. They have spent the night casting around for fish—discerning a call, to use contemporary language. What are they to become, now that they have been abandoned, as it seems, by the One they followed? Because the Beloved Disciple hears the voice of Jesus and Peter acts on it, the community discovers its direction.

We spend much time and energy protecting ourselves from others, in part because we understand that what others know about us, they can use against us. We use what we know against them, too. It is an unfortunate aspect of close community life that people will take advantage of what they know. If you are hurting, most people in the community will be there for you, but it too often happens that instead of helping the one who is hurting, we turn on him or her, almost instinctively, as animals go after the weakest prey. Yet if we are not naked with and attentive to each other, we cannot have community. We cannot be together if we keep secrets. It is one of the hardest truths of adult life—we have to shed light on the secrets that we hold most dear. It is at that moment of nakedness that we are most vulnerable—to hurt, yes, but also to healing. It is the prospect of healing that we most often lose sight of—the necessity of exposing ourselves to examination so that the hurt can be seen and healed.

Listening and nakedness are the essential attitudes of prayer. They are also the essential attitudes of service to others. That is what, in the end, we are called to discern—not the road to our personal happiness but to someone else's. If we are not naked and if we are not listening, we are not going to be available emotionally to those who need us. We will be turned inward in fear, anxiety, and self-pity. The emotion we want to awaken in our lives is to be directed toward someone else—

anger, love, desire, compassion—in order to awaken their deepest feelings. These are indicators of life itself, as well as the requirements of community.

My own experience of discerning the nature of my presence for others through listening and nakedness came through what is known as Clinical Pastoral Education, during which I worked in a hospital visiting the sick. I also met with others going through the same training to talk about what we felt when we encountered those who are sick or dying. We learned to listen to the sick so that we could know what they truly needed. We also learned to expose our own anxieties about sickness, our own fears of death. We learned to be naked with others so that we could more honestly care for them. This part of education for ministry is more important perhaps than other aspects of theological formation. When we talk about educating Christians, we often focus on how much people know about their faith, the Bible, the history of the church, while "outreach" ministries are important but relegated to the after-hours part of church life. But those who are sick or hurt do not usually need to hear about the historical Jesus and what theologians call his "radical table commensality"; they want someone to sit and eat with them, perhaps in silence, or to sit and listen to whatever they have to say without reservation or interruption. We have to learn how to do this, even in our own intimate relations. For some, even for devout Christians, it is a seemingly impossible task because in these encounters we have to expose ourselves.

I will never forget the first time I had to tell someone that he was going to die—and soon. This man was a member of my parish. When he was diagnosed with lung cancer, he was living in a single-room-occupancy hotel near my apartment in Manhattan. I became his primary caregiver, initially somewhat against my will. We had been taught not to become too emotionally involved in the lives of people in the parish, especially those like Walter who had drug-dependency problems. Such people were not trustworthy. But there was no one else to take care of Walter.

I became aware of his condition one Sunday when he prayed in church for healing. Afterwards, I asked him what was going on and, somewhat to my surprise, he poured out the story of having cancer. He asked me to go with him to the hospital for some tests. Later, I learned that he was also HIV positive. Over the next several months, Walter was in and out of the hospital frequently but always maintained that he was going to be fine, that God was going to cure him. I also learned that he had two brothers, on two coasts of the country, with whom he had lost contact. There were also daughters in the Northeast. He asked me to contact them and let them know his situation. Again, such deep involvement in a person's private life is tricky, but I decided that I had to do something to reconnect Walter to his family. As it happened, my efforts led to a reunion among Walter, one of his brothers, and his daughters a month before he died.

Walter and I could not have been more different. He had been in and out of jail, was a drug addict, and a mean drunk who disappeared regularly, and he may have been involved in drug trafficking. But at some level he had a deep need to be in touch with a church community and to be able to call it his. When we had breakfast on Saturday mornings, as we often did, he would speak emotionally about his church family and how it was all he really had. When he went into the hospital for the last time, I was there with him, and the doctors and nurses came to think of me as his primary family.

As I was leaving town to visit my parents before Christmas, I went to see Walter in the hospital and learned from his doctor that he would probably not be alive when I came back in a week. I decided to tell him that, to administer the last rites of the church, and to give him the eucharist. Although Walter and I had talked about dying—and not a month before I had discussed hospice care with him—he had not acknowledged that he would soon die. It was the unspoken truth between us that had to be said.

I sat by him on the bed. He was wearing an oxygen mask and breathing with difficulty. Looking deep into his eyes, I said: "Walter, we probably won't see each other again. You may die while I am away. And so I want to pray with you while we can and give you communion." His eyes grew wide, but he heard what I said. He saw that we were both naked in spirit and that this was love as palpable as he had ever known it. I read the "Ministration at the Time of Death" with him, anointed him with oil, and gave him communion. I prayed:

> Into your hands, O merciful Savior, we commend your servant, Walter. Acknowledge, we humbly beseech you, a sheep of your own fold, a lamb of your own flock, a sinner of your own redeeming. Receive him into the arms of your mercy, into the blessed rest of everlasting peace, and into the glorious company of the saints in light. May his soul and the souls of all the departed, through the mercy of God, rest in peace. Amen.

In my experience it is unusual to say this prayer for someone who is conscious at the time, but I felt deeply connected to Walter. The prayer was for both of us a beautiful reminder of our communion. I too am part of that flock and one who is redeemed. I too look toward arms of mercy, a blessed rest, and the saints in light. We share this common end, as did Jesus and the disciples who saw him standing on the shore of the lake. His presence suggested that they shared more than a common death, however.

Walter and I said goodbye when we had finished our prayer. He said, "I love you," as he always did when I left him. He held his arms open to embrace me. The day after Christmas the hospital called to tell me he was dead. I called his brother. A month later I received in the mail a photograph that Walter's brother had taken of the two of us in the hospital when he and Walter's daughters had visited. It is, to my mind, a photograph of what it means to be in Christian community. Walter is gaunt, almost skeletal, but he is smiling. His arm is around me. His pajamas are loose on his frame. Beside him, I am almost pudgy. My arm is around him, and I am also smiling. In not that many years, I will also be dead.

When Peter jumps into the water to swim toward Jesus, he is reclaiming something he lost when he denied that he knew the man on trial before Rome. The other disciples haul in the catch of fish and continue to beat toward the shore. They are not far from the place where Jesus is standing, and the catch is too good to lose. They go on working in the presence of someone who has risen from the dead. It is in many ways a remarkable response. But it carries a deep truth.

In the presence of life and death, in the sight of God, we continue to be who we are, but when we know ourselves to be in God we are more abundantly ourselves. We do not automatically know that God is with us. Jesus came to show us that in the most graphic way possible: by living wholly, dying unjustly, and returning joyfully. His is the model for human life: not because he redeems human life (gives it meaning) but because he reveals it as it truly is, as we truly are. That is the nature of his saving grace.

The skills we need in order to live more faithfully in community are those of our human nature. They are the primary attitudes basic to growth in the spirit. They mark this dimension of spiritual life as fundamental to everything else that comes later. The task is to be in this almost constant state of discernment, of listening in naked silence to the spirit. I have often found that where I am spiritually is shown to me in dreams. These are not dreams about the future. They are very much about the present. When my prayer life is good—when I am practicing spirituality in a regular way—my dreams are clarifying. They are filled with signs of the spirit. The effect is like that of entering into Scripture with active imagination.

On a recent night between Holy Saturday and Easter morning, I dreamed that I was going to meet a professional colleague at her house, but when I got there I discovered that it was falling apart. The roof had collapsed. The wooden siding had begun to rot. The porch had fallen in. There was clearly no one living there. I walked around and through the house and saw no one. I then went outside and saw, through woods next to the house, a beautiful river that flowed through a ravine into a lake. There was a light mist rising from the river. In the dream I said, "I want that river." I felt the pull of its beauty, which I have felt in other circumstances as an angler approaching a river in the mountains. Such scenes always make me ache with what can only be called desire. This vision of a river was one of wanting, of desire.

I then found myself in a barn or shed near the tumbled-down house. Stepping toward the door to go back outside, I realized that there was something waiting for me on the other side. I felt this expectation as dread, but I said, "Lift the shadow of the earth." Opening the door, I saw darkness and knew that something was coming toward me from the dark. It terrified me, but at the same time I stepped toward it, calling out. My call came from my throat as a moan that woke me up, but in the dream I was not running away from, nor attacking, what was coming toward me. I wanted what was coming out of the dark, just as I had wanted that river in the woods.

This was for me a profound Easter dream and not unlike what the disciples are experiencing as they row and swim toward Jesus on the shore. His presence there is both a product of their own desire and a terrifying possibility. They want it and at the same time fear it. Their own readiness has made his presence possible and real, just as my own spiritual work made my dream possible. Two months before this dream my father died, and a year earlier I had ended a relationship with someone connected to the person I was to meet in that broken-down house. The dream was a sign of my need to step into the future that awaits after resurrection, to reach for the one who comes out of the dark after a long night of isolation, even though the vision of new life is surprisingly terrifying.

One of the reasons we are uneasy with the kind of discernment required by mature spiritual life is that when we are naked and listening for our life's truth, we will certainly encounter more than we expect or even want. Resurrection has to be painful, not only for the one who comes back but for those who welcome back the dead. What news does this man on the shore bring to them? What does he know that they may not be ready to hear? How will their lives change in that knowledge?

Peter swims toward revelation. I see him crawling, splashing onto the shore where Jesus is smiling, laughing at him. He sits on his haunches, spitting water and sand, breathing hard. Jesus looks past him at the boat with its bulky net of fish wallowing toward them. Peter looks too. It is like old times, all of them on the shore of the lake hauling in fish for the morning market. Peter thinks for a moment that it will be like old times. Nothing has really changed. Nothing has to change. I suspect that all of us react in the same way to revelation. First, we are relieved that all will be well. And, second, we conclude that if all will be well nothing will change. When Peter looks back at Jesus, he sees in the face of the man he thought he knew something quite different. Coming out of the dark of the night is something he wants and fears. He hears the boat hit the sand behind him, the splash of feet into the water, the flapping of the fish in the heavy net, loud breathing, the wash of wavelets.

The end of discernment is to discover how nothing will be the same again, how change is the constant of the spiritual journey.

Chapter 3

"Come, Have Breakfast"

9 When they had gone ashore, they saw a charcoal fire there, with fish on it, and bread. 10 Jesus said to them, "Bring some of the fish that you have just caught." 11 So Simon Peter went aboard and hauled the net ashore. It was full of large fish, a hundred fifty-three of them; and though there were so many, the net was not torn. 12 Jesus said to them, "Come have breakfast." Now none of the disciples dared to ask him, "Who are you?" because they knew it was the Lord. 13 Jesus came and took the bread and gave it to them, and did the same with the fish. 14 This was now the third time that Jesus appeared to the disciples after he was raised from the dead.

I picture Jesus as a fly fisherman—and more than that, a catch-and-release angler who uses barbless hooks: what he takes out of the water he puts back.[1] He appreciates the subtleties of the sport, the serenity of the river. He understands the Zen of fly casting, the intimate connection between angler and living water that rests on the

---

1. Norman Maclean in his story, *A River Runs Through It* makes a similar connection between religion and fishing that some readers will recall: "In our family, there was no clear line between religion and fly fishing. We lived at the junction of great trout rivers in western Montana, and our father was a Presbyterian minister and a fly fisherman. . . . He told us about Christ's

slender line. The game is not about killing fish. I cannot see Jesus baiting hooks with night crawlers or gutting a trout by the stream, as if he were a character in a Hemingway story. But if he did kill a fish, he would have killed it not for himself but to feed others, as he does here on the shore of Lake Tiberias.

Fly fishing at night is at the primal heart of angling: casting in the dark is both an act of faith and the epitome of skill. It summons mystery, which materializes as the fish. I used to fish after midnight for striped bass on the Rhode Island shore, in Quonochontaug Pond. A breach way connected the saltwater pond to the ocean. The bass would come in on the tide to feed. I positioned myself at the mouth of the breach way and cast my fly (a feathered lure, known as a "deceiver," designed to resemble a baitfish) upstream and near the opposite bank. The incoming tide carried it down past me in a long arc to the pond where the bass were usually feeding. Often I saw their dark long bodies shooting through the shallows.

On one occasion, I kept up this casting rhythm for an hour but caught nothing—not at all an unusual experience. I was standing in the pond at the edge of the current and could feel the strength of the water against my waders. It was a good feeling, one of life, not danger, even though the bottom dropped off precipitously in front of me. While I cast, I thought of nothing, my mind as empty as the sky above me. This emptiness is a condition of spiritual grace, what we search for in meditation but have so much trouble

---

disciples being fishermen, and we were left to assume, as my brother and I did, that all first-class fishermen on the Sea of Galilee were fly fishermen and that John, the favorite, was a dry-fly fisherman." (Chicago: The University of Chicago Press, 1976), p. 1.

achieving because our minds will not stop searching for
something to do. Somehow, the repetitive act of casting and retrieving a fly stills the restless mind. It is as
good a reason to fish as any.

When the disciples get out of the boat on the beach,
Jesus already has a fish on the fire. When I ask myself
where he got it, I suddenly see him with a fly rod on
the shore of Tiberias, perhaps at the place where the
Jordan flows in. He has a good stroke. The line unfolds
in an easy almost lazy parabola. He snaps the rod forward with just the right amount of wrist. The line
unrolls, hangs a moment in the night, and alights with
a whisper on the surface of the lake. He strips it slowly
in. Do the fish take every time Jesus casts? I do not think
so. He would not enjoy fishing if there were no effort
or skill involved. He might even curse the missed strike,
the quick fish that spits out the lure before he can
tighten the line. But he is always awake, as is the fish.

When I fish, I am attentive but not always awake.
As in prayer, we have to be awake in order to make the
connection. Jesus knows that. He probably does not
wear his robes while he fishes. In fact, I think he is
naked by Tiberias, even as Peter is naked out in the
boat where they cannot see each other. He casts his fly
over and over again, thinking of nothing, in complete
harmony with what is.

The fish struck, as fish often do, as my fly reached
the end of its drift and stopped abruptly, rising in the
current. The bass that took it hit hard. It felt like a fist
against my arm. My rod bent into a u-shape and the
fish began to run against the current and then, confused by the bite of the hook, turned downstream. It
was hard to fight the fish against the fast tide, and I
did not want to exhaust it. I tried to lead it out of the

current into the quiet shallows, wading along the sharp drop off, following the fish as it strained against the line. It felt like a big one, maybe big enough to keep. At that time, there were limits on the size of bass that could be killed, twenty-eight inches long. That is a big fish, although many striped bass are forty or fifty inches in length and can weigh sixty or more pounds. This one was not that big.

I think that the fish Jesus caught for the disciples—however he got it—was legal. It was probably several pounds, maybe even ten. This was not a small fish. Everyone would have enough to eat. (Remember, however, that in this same spot, or at least nearby, Jesus fed five thousand with two small fish.) Jesus drags it ashore after a good fight and prepares it for cooking, draping a loincloth around his hips. He expresses his gratitude to the fish and to God for bringing it to him. As a country boy, he knows how to slit the fish and clean out its guts. He cooks it with the head on. I can see him kneeling by the shore working on this fish, knowing that soon the disciples will come into view. The fire is already going and soon there will be a nice bed of coals for cooking. Jesus is hungry. He spreads the two sides of the gutted fish on stakes and positions it over the coals. Right away he can smell the cooking flesh, and his mouth waters. He turns around, sees the fishing boat dimly emerging on the dark lake, and waves.

My fish was too short to keep. It lay gasping on the sand, looking at me with a terrified eye. Both of us were tired, but the fish was in danger and I was not. I had to return him quickly to the water or he would die. I held him at the edge of the current, my left hand under his belly, my right hand holding his tail. I moved him

back and forth to push the water through his gills. And
then released him. He disappeared quickly into the
pond. The next morning my in-laws were astonished
that I had not kept the fish. They wanted to know how
long it was. I thought it was about twenty-six inches.
Only two inches too short! Who would know if you
kept such a fish? It was close enough.

Jesus would have thrown it back, I am sure of that.
This is one of the answers to the question, What would
Jesus do? He would not keep fish under the legal limit,
even if they were only an inch too short, to feed himself. On the other hand, he might keep an illegal fish
to feed others.

The disciples come ashore. Peter has arrived ahead
of them, soaking wet. He warms himself by the charcoal fire, just as he warmed himself by the fire in a
courtyard in Jerusalem not too many days before. The
fish is broiling over the fire. It is different from those
the other disciples are bringing in. Jesus feeds us even
though we already have more than we need. There is
no scarcity here.

The eucharist is at the heart of the third dimension
of the journey toward wisdom that I want to discuss in
this chapter: transformation. The breakfast that Jesus
prepares for the disciples is a eucharist that gathers into
one meal Israel's experience of God's plenty. Jesus
called this the kingdom of heaven. In this ritual enactment, we encounter the scriptural roots of the sacrament that unites all Christians across time to Israel, to
one another, and to the Risen Christ. In meeting the
Christ in one another, we are invited to be changed.
But how does that happen? What does this story in
John 21 tell us about this encounter with Christ?

The transformation wrought by God in this act of eating together is not merely personal. Our transformative encounter with God in Christ is meant to change everything, not only ourselves. It prophetically affirms Israel's experience of the Creator who continues to be part of creation, inviting us to enter into creative partnership as co-creators. The roots of eucharist are in the whole of salvation history. They originate in the Hebrew Scriptures: the Exodus, Joseph in Egypt, Ezekiel and the renewal of creation. That is why all of salvation history is recounted in some form in the prayers we hear at the eucharist and is present in the act of communion. In the same way, this scene in John 21 echoes an earlier story in John 6, the feeding of the five thousand by Lake Tiberias. It was near the time of Passover; Jesus went up on a mountain with the disciples. The crowd followed him, and he asked Philip where they might buy bread to feed them all. The discussion that follows is about scarcity—the lack of money to buy enough bread, the small amount of barley loaves and fish (only two) that a boy has brought. Jesus gives thanks for the bread: the Greek word used is *eucharistesas*. [2]

When they have eaten and gathered up the leftovers in twelve baskets (surely representing the twelve tribes of Israel), we are meant to remember an earlier meal that takes place in the wilderness, recounted in Exodus 16:16, where manna is gathered for the people of Israel in the desert. Sufficient for one day, this manna falls upon the dew in the night. It was thought to descend like rain, as Moses sings in Deuteronomy 32:2-3:

2. In 2 Kings 4:42-44, the prophet Elisha also feeds the hungry—with twenty loaves of barley.

May my teaching drop like the rain,
my speech condense like the dew;
like gentle rain on grass,
like showers on new growth.

And so one might call this manna bread from heaven,
which, like Jesus, is the word that becomes flesh.

The echoes continue. Jesus feeds the five thousand
shortly before the feast of the Passover—and like
this feeding of the people of Israel in the desert it is
a reminder of the liberation from Egypt. After the
people of Israel crossed the Jordan and ate the
Passover in the Promised Land for the first time, we
read in Joshua 5:11-12 that: "On the day after the
passover, on that very day, they ate the produce of the
land, unleavened cakes and parched grain. The
manna ceased on the day they ate the produce of the
land."

Following the feeding of the multitudes in John 6,
the disciples get into a boat and begin to row across
the lake, leaving Jesus behind. It is dark, as it is in John
21, and the sea becomes rough. Suddenly, they see
Jesus coming toward them, walking on the water. They
"receive" him and instantly are transported to the other
shore. The disciples want to know what happened.
Jesus tells them that they were seeking him because
they were well fed. "Do not work for the food that per-
ishes," he admonishes them, "but for the food that
endures for eternal life, which the Son of Man will give
you." They want to know by what sign they are to recognize that Jesus is the one who gives eternal life, and
Jesus tells them:

"Our ancestors ate the manna in the wilderness; as it
is written, 'He gave them bread from heaven to eat.'"

Then Jesus said to them, "Very truly, I tell you, it was not Moses who gave you the bread from heaven, but it is my Father who gives you the true bread from heaven. For the bread of God is that which comes down from heaven and gives life to the world." They said to him, "Sir, give us this bread always." Jesus said to them, "I am the bread of life. Whoever comes to me will never be hungry, and whoever believes in me will never be thirsty" (Jn. 6:31-35).

Following a time of fallowness—the long night on the water or forty years in the desert—comes a time of abundance. Perhaps we are to recall the story of Joseph and the alternating years of famine and plenty in Egypt that lead to the enslavement and liberation of the people of Israel. Or perhaps we are just to notice this pattern in our history with God. There are days of abundance and days of want: but the underlying goodness of God is always there. There are fish in the water even if we do not see or catch them. This is also the pattern in our own lives.

Our eucharistic meal today does not include fish, but it appears that the common meal of the early church did—and not only as the main course but as a food with ritual importance. The fish is significant in Christian history as a symbol of Christ, of the newly baptized, and of the eucharist. One of the church fathers, Tertullian, referred to the newly baptized as "little fishes," who follow Big Fish—a connection with the idea of second birth in the waters of Baptism. The Greek word ΙΧΘΥΣ (ichthus) may also have suggested to early Christians an acrostic derived from the Greek letters in this word for fish: Ιησους Χριστος Θεος Υιος Σωτηρ (Jesus Christ, Son of God, Savior). Most

important for our purpose here is that in the fourth and
fifth centuries, the fish became an explicit emblem of
the eucharist and is frequently found in catacomb
paintings associated with bread and wine. Fish, bread,
and wine are also important in Jewish history and practice, and we need always to bear in mind that Jesus in
performing these ritual actions as a Jew. Those who are
with him are Jews, and the writers of the Gospels are,
for the most part, writing in a Jewish context. The
Gospel writers evoke Jewish tradition when they
describe the feeding of the multitudes or provide not
only bread but fish for them. The use of the image of
the vine, as I mentioned earlier, also recalls the relationship between the people of Israel and God as the
vine-grower.

The eucharist recapitulates the entirety of this relationship as it is portrayed in Scripture. This moment
on the shore, as Jesus prepares breakfast for the disciples, is likewise meant to be seen as a manifestation of
God's presence as revealed in Scripture. It is an act of
thanksgiving, a feast of Passover, a eucharist.

Even though Jesus has a fish on the grill, he asks
Peter to haul in the catch of fish: "Bring some of the
fish that you have just caught." Despite the size of the
catch, the net does not break. Jesus then invites the disciples to join him for breakfast. Some commentators
have suggested that this scene is really about bringing
in new converts for the church: Peter hauls in sinners
who need saving. The number of fish cited is a subject
of extended debate. Some say that there were one hundred and fifty-three species of fish identified at that
time, and therefore this number represents the idea of
bringing all of creation to Christ. Others argue that
Peter's taking charge and hauling in the net by himself

is an acknowledgment of his ecclesial authority. In other words, a church unified under his leadership will bring more converts.

When we bring people to Christ, however, I do not think we entrap them in nets and haul them in whether they want to come or not. Nor do we intend to cook and eat them when we invite them to our table. They are not the main course. Unfortunately, the church has in its history brought people to the table in order to consume them—and this vision of ministry as a hunting and gathering mission is all too common. Jesus brought people to his table in order to share God's plenty with them, not to deprive them of their liberty. He wants everyone, not only those already in church, to have life and have it more abundantly.

What, then, do we make of this enormous catch of fish, the unbroken net, the emphasis on dragging it ashore even though Jesus has already prepared the meal? Peter does perform a prodigious act in pulling the net ashore by himself (especially after the disciples in the boat have had trouble managing the large catch). The kind of net needed to catch so many fish is called a trammel, which one person would be unable to bring ashore. The trammel was used especially for night fishing. It comes in units about one hundred and fifteen feet long and five feet high. Ordinarily, several units would be tied together to form a fence at the bottom of the lake. The fishermen would splash water with their oars to drive fish into the net. It appears that what the disciples were using when Jesus asked them to cast to the right side of the boat was a throw net—too small for such a large catch. The story does not make practical sense, from a fishing perspective.

The story is not about fishing, however; in that sense, the details do not matter. The story is about transformation in eucharist. Transformation requires that one thing be changed into another. What is being changed into what? Peter and the disciples come to Jesus bringing themselves and a large catch of fish. In sharing the meal with him, they become agents of change for the world, co-creators. There is a passage in the Hebrew Scriptures that helps orient us to this meaning. In it we can see why fish and water and this gathering on the shore are important to understanding the mission of Jesus and the church, as it was seen by the author of John 21. The passage is in Ezekiel.

Ezekiel 47 contains a description of the renewed temple for the postexilic community, those Jews who have returned from Babylon to rebuild their lives in Judea. It is a vision of the ideal relationship between Israel and Yahweh for the future, captured in Ezekiel's description of the sacred river flowing in all directions from the temple. This figure is found in the book of Revelation as well: "the river of the water of life, bright as crystal, flowing from the throne of God and of the Lamb through the middle of the street of the city" (22:1–2). This is the one river running through the Bible from Genesis to Revelation. Ezekiel is taken to the bank of this river, and Yahweh asks, "Mortal, have you seen this?"

> This water flows toward the eastern region and goes down into the Arabah; and when it enters the sea, the sea of stagnant waters, the water will become fresh. Wherever the river goes, every living creature that swarms will live, and there will be very many fish, once these waters reach there. It will become fresh; and

everything will live where the river goes. People will stand fishing beside the sea. . . . it will be a place for the spreading of nets; its fish will be of a great many kinds, like the fish of the Great Sea (Ezek. 47:6–10).

This is the great catch of fish that is at the heart of Jesus' encounter with the disciples on the beach. In both Ezekiel and Revelation the effects of this river of living water are described as the flourishing of all kinds of trees and flowering plants, echoing in both cases the description of the Garden of Eden in Genesis. It is about the renewal of creation, just as the eucharist is.

The salt waters of the Dead Sea are freshened; the desolate wilderness of Judah becomes fruitful, creating a new paradise for those who have returned from exile (and for those who have been raised from the dead). Far from being an image of capturing, converting, or gathering people, this picture of the great catch of fish in John 21 is a reaffirmation of the presence of the glory of God, from whose throne (in whose presence) all things are made new. The dead lake from which no fish came is suddenly alive with every kind of fish there is. Its fecundity is beyond human imagining. The disciples who have been in exile following the death of Jesus are offered a new vision of a new heaven and a new earth, one that is full of plenty.[3]

3. This vision does not replace Ezekiel's. For the people of Israel returning from exile, the building of a new Temple reaffirmed their identity. In this chapter of John, and for the Jewish Christians struggling with their identity as followers of Christ, the Resurrection reaffirms the continuing presence of God. Given that the Temple had also been destroyed two decades before this gospel was written, the story is also a reaffirmation of the Temple as a spiritual entity. It has not been destroyed. I am not suggesting here that Jesus replaces the Temple, as if to say that Christianity replaces Judaism. The writer of this chapter is still speaking in a Jewish context and writing a form of midrash that does not deny but affirms the experience of Israel.

The eucharist, then, is both continuity and change. It is rooted here in Israel's relationship with Yahweh, as recounted in Scripture, and looks forward to a new configuration of community that renews but does not replace the covenant relationship with God. The eucharist transforms us into the beloved community. Through it we die and are reborn, as the people of Israel were and as Jesus was.

In the critical encounter on the shore, the disciples meet the numinous. They have a direct experience of the presence of God and are transformed, as we are. One way we meet the divine is in Scripture, as we have seen, where our reality as readers or hearers of the Word is shown to be God's. John 21 is one of the places in which we can see the Risen Christ. The experience can be that vivid. We are there on the shore with Jesus and the disciples—and what happens to them happens to us. When we read the Gospel in worship, we encounter Christ, just as we do in sharing the eucharist. Both activities are central to Christian practice. Through them we are fed by Christ and come to know more clearly who we are called to be. We receive the nourishment to do the work of adulthood, to build community, to feed and care for each other. In the Gospel and eucharistic presence of Jesus, we are changed—and our relationships with others are also changed. We begin, in this most intimate of encounters with the Lord, to open ourselves to others. These are not private acts—hearing the Gospel, sharing the eucharist—nor are they restricted privileges. They ground a common way of life.

Jesus' life was marked by the radical table fellowship that is presented in the gospels as such a scandal in his time. He came eating and drinking. He was called a glutton, a party-goer who mixed with the lowest classes in society. He spoke of abolishing privilege and preference. I come, he said, as a servant; the one who is last shall be first. The strong final eucharistic image of John's Gospel is that moment on the cross when Jesus' side is pierced by a spear and water and blood flow out. His body is given completely, and the Spirit is born of water and blood to enliven the community, represented by the Beloved Disciple and Mary at the foot of the cross. They represent the new communal (eucharistic) order that Jesus serves.

The Gospel of John does not include, as the other gospels do, the institution of the Last Supper as a ritual of remembrance. The last gathering of the disciples is not a Passover meal. Instead, Jesus washes the disciples' feet, taking the role of a servant. He explains to them, "For I have set you an example, that you also should do as I have done to you" (John 13:15). He then goes on to speak of the inner life of the community that lives as one body and one vine, abiding in love. This is the essence of the eucharistic community modeled in the Gospel of John. What is important is not the bread and the wine—or the bread and the fish. It does not matter what we do, or what we eat, when we come together. What matters is the One in whose name we gather.

For awhile I was a consultant to a Presbyterian congregation in Manhattan on the nature of its diaconal ministry. The project culminated in a Maundy Thursday service that was designed to gather up in one liturgical event the themes of *diakonia* (the New Testament word for servanthood) that had motivated our time together. The Maundy Thursday service, which traditionally memorializes the institution of the Last Supper as sacrament, incorporates the church's only foot-washing liturgy. Many denominations, among them the Presbyterian Church, do not routinely include the actual washing of feet in the service. Hand washing is occasionally substituted, which avoids the truth at the heart of the ritual.

Working together, the deacons at the church organized an agape meal (a simple feast of soup, bread, cheese, and fruit), to which we invited the residents of a single-room-occupancy building next to the church. The evening was to include Taizé-style chanting, the washing of feet, and the meal; everyone sat at a u-shaped table. The dinner was the liturgy, as indeed it was when Jesus brought the disciples together for their last supper before his execution. The pastor sat on a chair in the center and washed the feet of those who wished to come forward. Then a blessing was said over the meal that had the ritual cadence of a eucharistic prayer but was not a consecration. What was being blessed in this event was not only the food but also the gathering itself. We were all marked as holy.

Only two people came from the single-room-occupancy hotel next to the church, and that was disappointing. We had wanted to open the walls of the church in a way that mirrored the open-table ministry of Jesus in his own time. One of the members of the congregation went out into the street and brought back two homeless men she knew. They came in, took plates of bread and cheese and a bowl of soup, and left. A twelve-step program was meeting in the church, and the pastor invited them to come for soup following their meeting. For awhile nothing happened. Then, as we were clearing the tables and washing the dishes, six men came in.

"We hear that you have free food," one of them said.

"We do," answered Barbara, the deacon who had invited the homeless men. She set the table for these newcomers. "Just sit," she said. "We'll serve you."

Barbara and my fiancée Connie brought the six men their soup and bread, poured tea and coffee, then stayed to chat. It was all very simple. The rest of us were in the kitchen washing dishes. As they were leaving, I heard one of the men say to the two women, "You are both angels."

The feeding of the congregation and the six visitors was the essence of eucharist. In this ritual, members of the church discovered new dimensions to their own sense of what it means to be in community. They were changed in serving and being served. No one there realized that the meal they shared was a eucharist. It did not fit their definition of that liturgy, not only because the shape of the event was more like supper with friends—not at all solemn—but also because it included real food meant for consumption. All food and all people may be consecrated in eucharist: cheese, bread, soup, Christians, non-Christian, us, them.

This encounter at the table, as community, is transformative. We are turned around by it. After we have eaten, after we have washed each other's feet, we are new creations. It is here, however, that we often get stuck—coming to the table in private devotion and returning to our pews unchanged. This is partly the result of our limited vision of what happens in the eucharist or in worship. Many imagine that the priest is doing something powerful *for* us, somehow converting the bread and wine into the body and blood of a magical Christ, so that when I take the elements into my mouth I am ingesting Christ, who fuels me for the struggle against evil. I am helped to be a better person, perhaps. I am saved by edification: it is mostly about me and my personal experience. It is about my being given eternal life, which otherwise I am presumed to lack. This vision of eucharist does not change me, however. It is more like taking an antibiotic regularly, as prescribed. I think that it also is rooted in an attitude of submission to the power of the church rather than in the partnership of equals taught and exemplified by Jesus.

The problem with this theology is that it makes us into passive recipients of grace. It is a distortion of that doctrine into what Dietrich Bonhoeffer called "cheap grace." With such grace, nothing is changed. It is grace, as Bonhoeffer puts it, "as the church's inexhaustible pantry, from which it is doled out by careless hands without hesitation or limit. It is grace without a price, without costs . . . a cheap coverup . . . a denial of God's living word, denial of the incarnation of the word of God."[4] Grace is not private, as Bonhoeffer's life showed. As does the death of Christ, it forces us sometimes to face unpleasant truths about the world.

Jesus dies as a victim of injustice, as so many do, and God is with him as God is with all victims—and with us. The Resurrection is the sign of that unwavering presence. God does not sacrifice Jesus to prove a point, nor to make me feel better about myself. God does not sacrifice Jesus at all. Jesus dies by the hand of tyranny— a Jew killed not by Jews but by Romans. Once we see his death in that way, it is difficult, I think, to speak of

---

4. Dietrich Bonhoeffer, *Discipleship* (Minneapolis, MN: Fortress Press, Dietrich Bonhoeffer Works, volume 4, 2001), p. 43

salvation as being primarily about my personally living forever. Nor is his life and death about the failure of Judaism.

While it may be true that the eucharist will help me in my struggles to be myself, to resist temptation, its real power is elsewhere. First, as a community, we bring to the table our gifts—bread and wine, money and food—or in the case of this story in John, a net full of fish. We bring gifts from the bounty of creation. We bring the gift of ourselves, who are also creation's plenty. In the Great Thanksgiving, in the prayer of consecration, these gifts are lifted up, as we are lifted up, to be visible signs of the holy. We are not made holy. We already are sanctified. What the eucharist does is show us to ourselves. We are the body and blood. We are united in one body, which is revealed as divine, just as in his body Jesus was revealed as divine. We are like him in all ways. This is not a private act. It is not about my salvation or my living forever. It is about the sanctity of all things in their common holiness. That is one of the reasons priests are not allowed to celebrate the eucharist without at least one other person present. Once, the celebration of the Mass was about the priest, acting for the community. Now, it is about the community acting for God.

So we are sanctified as community, in the name of Jesus who modeled this way of life for us. And this community is one of strangers, as he also demonstrated. It is not a family gathering. Here is another misconception that stunts our growth as Christians—that we come together as a family of intimates. Orthodox belief can often have this side effect: that we are insiders who know how the game is played. In the pre-Vatican II church, for example, one progressed up a ladder of orders to deacon, at which point one might touch the consecrated elements. This is an idea of the sacred that has made Christianity for many an unattractive, exclusionary club that they do not want to join. We forget the stranger who does not know our ways. It also emphasizes revelation as hidden, an oxymoron if there ever was one. The Orthodox and Roman Catholic churches still turn away from communion those who are not officially admitted to their rites. The Episcopal Church—with the exception of a few parishes—turns away only those who are not baptized. Jesus, of course, turned away no one. When we fed our visitors at the Maundy Thursday service, we did not ask if they were baptized.

Although the transformation wrought in the eucharist is communal, social, what changes is my very understanding of who I am. As Jesus suggests when he washes the disciples' feet, we are called in this community to give ourselves up to others, to lose ourselves. In our culture, resistance to this imperative is fierce, even though it is taught not only by Christianity but by the other major world religions as well. Knowing the true self is to lose the self. One reason for that seemingly paradoxical truth is that as we come to know ourselves, we inevitably come to understand that others are like us and that our well-being depends fundamentally on theirs.

As a deacon in the Episcopal Church, one of my liturgical responsibilities is to clean up after communion. In some parishes, this cleanup is done on the altar; in other places, it is done in the sacristy. Although it is not in itself a particularly sacred act, there is something profound about it. I collect the plates and brush whatever breadcrumbs are on them into a chalice. I pour the leftover consecrated wine into that same chalice (unless there is a lot of it, in which case it is reserved). Everyone in the congregation has sipped wine from the common cup. Mixed into this remaining concoction is the saliva of all of the people in the church. As we pass the cup from one to another, the wine becomes a richer blend of our lives. Everyone is present in the same chalice. Every time I look into the cup I think of that, give thanks, and then consume whatever is there. I drink it all. It is the strongest image I know of what it means for a community to be united in faith. It also emphasizes the importance of our physical being with one another, as did Jesus' Resurrection. Most clergy would say, I think, that we treat the leftover bread and wine with reverence because the elements are or, represent, the body and blood of Christ. I prefer to reverence the community that has been united in the cup.

The great catch of fish mingles all kinds in one net. They are all brought to the table as signs of creation's goodness. The net does not break, even though we in the church often fear that the stranger, especially a lot of strangers, will break us. In the same way, when Jesus feeds the multitudes, he does not ask who these people are or if any of them has properly prepared to join in the feast. He simply feeds them all.

"Come and have breakfast," Jesus says to those who have come ashore bringing God's bounty in their nets. There is, however, an odd moment in verse 12. In response to Jesus' invitation, the gospel writer tells us, the disciples do not dare to ask "Who are you?" because "they knew it was the Lord." It is the second time in this chapter that the disciples have been uneasy about the identity of the one who has called and is feeding them.

This question of who Jesus is goes to the heart of the Gospel of John, which at one level is a lengthy explanation of his identity. As the Prologue to John's Gospel says: He is, from the beginning, "the Word" who was with God. Although "all things came into being through him," the world did not know him. All who received him, however, received "power to become children of God." So "the Word became flesh and lived among us," and "we have seen his glory, . . . full of grace and truth." "From his fullness we have all received, grace upon grace." It is this one, called by John's community the Son of God, who has made God known. This is the mysterious Christ that the Gospel seeks to present through the signs that show him to the faithful.

The question might be reframed in this way. The disciples look at the one who was dead and now seems to them to be very alive, offering them breakfast at dawn. The first question that has to occur to them is: Who are you? You look like the one we knew who was crucified, but he is dead. That was in Jerusalem. Here we are now in this other place, in what seems to be another life, and now you are here, not exactly as we knew you and yet so much like the one we loved. Who are you? The question is equally about the community: Who are we whose identity was so connected to yours?

The question is not one they can ask aloud, perhaps because, as the text says, they know he is not the one they knew before. They know that he is the Lord, a new creation, who, because of their relationship to him in community, opens to them life as a new creation. As Paul wrote in 2 Corinthians 5:17, "if anyone is in Christ, there is a new creation: everything old has passed away; see, everything has become new!" If Jesus

has changed, have we also changed? What are we called
to be now? This is the essential question we encounter
in this dimension of our spiritual practice. We put ourselves at risk every time we enter into worship together
or begin to pray. In these acts, we allow our ideas of
ourselves to be challenged, our preconceptions about
the world to be proved wrong, and our plans to be
overturned.

Each of us who has lost a parent or child or loved
one has had an experience like this. Looking at the one
who has died—or at the coffin or urn that contains him
or her, or even at a picture—the inevitable question is:
Who are you? And, now that you are gone, who am I?
When my father died at eighty-one he had suffered
from Parkinson's disease for fifteen years. Although he
had changed in many ways during the course of his illness, he was the same man I had grown up with and
with whom I had had a difficult relationship. His death
changed my perception of myself. I could no longer
define myself according to his expectations, although
consciously I had ceased to do that years ago. The
nature of our relationship has changed, however. Following his death, I am solely responsible for it. At the
same time I cannot expunge him from my identity. I
have to accommodate his continuing presence.

The day after his funeral, my mother and I, my two
sisters, and my fiancée were sitting around the dining
room table looking at old photographs. It was a good
way to pass the time together and to remind ourselves
of who we are as a family. My mother came to one photograph of my father from 1945 when they lived in Ari-
zona. She smiled and picked up the photo. Turning
suddenly to me she said, "This was taken right after
you came back from the war." We were all stunned. She

looked confused for a moment and then, remembering that he was dead, began to cry. In that instant, I understood that the question of his identity was also about my own. So it is with the disciples and with us who follow Jesus now. In asking who he is, we are also asking who we are. If we ask in earnest, we expose our lives to fundamental change.

Once Jesus has fed them, the text tells us that "this was now the third time that Jesus appeared to the disciples after he was raised from the dead." The previous two appearances are in Chapter 20:19–23 and 26-29, when Jesus appears to the disciples as a gathered community on "the first day of the week," the day on which Christians had probably begun to celebrate the Lord's Supper. The purpose of these visits seems to be to verify who he is. Jesus shows them the wounds in his hands and his side. The one who was crucified is also the one standing before them. It is no hoax. In the second appearance, he allows Thomas to touch the wounds, saying, "Do not doubt but believe." Thomas cries out, "My Lord and my God!"

In both instances Jesus empowers the community to continue to do his work. He breathes the Holy Spirit upon them and claims that those who do not see but still believe are blessed of God. The hearers of the Gospel of John, those in the Johannine community, were hearers of the Word who believed that they were guided by the Holy Spirit. These accounts of the resurrected Jesus affirm that they live in the power and security of the Spirit and that those who have told them that Jesus died and rose again are trustworthy witnesses.

This third appearance is different. Jesus does not say that he is the crucified one, nor does he show the disciples his wounds. The text says that he eats the bread and fish with them, as he does in Luke 24:43. His presence calls the community into being after the long night of despair and uncertainty. This appearance verifies who the disciples are, not who Jesus is. What their meal together affirms, following the catch of fish that is a sign of new creation, is that in Jesus they will know themselves. The rest of John 21 is about the nature of that knowing. The meal is the prelude to their deeper call to discipleship that issues from this transforming encounter with Jesus.

As with the disciples at Emmaus, our eyes are opened in the act of breaking bread with one another. At Emmaus the disciples recognized Jesus, whom they were prevented (by their own blindness) from seeing until the Scriptures had been explained to them. Here, the disciples recognize each other as part of a community in formation. The story is about the birth of the church as a separate entity that takes only Jesus as its spiritual leader. But what makes this chapter so interesting is that it also leads beyond Jesus. What is resurrected is much more than a single person.

If we take another look at the experience that Mary has in the garden on that first day of the week when she went to the tomb, we can see more clearly where this final chapter of John might be taking us. Both Peter and the Beloved Disciple go to look at the empty tomb when Mary tells them, "They have taken the Lord out of the tomb." They run to see what has happened. The disciple whom Jesus loved gets to the tomb first and, looking in at the abandoned linen wrappings, believes—although we are not told *what* he believes. The two disciples go home, leaving Mary behind.

She is weeping and then sees two angels who ask her why she weeps. Because, she says, they have taken my Lord and I don't know where they have laid him. After she says this, she turns around and sees Jesus, except that she does not know that it is Jesus. Supposing him to be the gardener, she asks where he has taken the body. Jesus then calls her by name, "Mary," and at that she turns (again) and calls him, in Hebrew, "Rabbouni," or teacher. She now knows who is with her. She recognizes the one who had been crucified—although here there is no proof of identity required. Mary knows who this man is because he knows who she is.

Mary turns. She experiences a change, what we might call *metanoia*—a reversal of direction, a conversion. She no longer weeps for the one who is gone nor for herself, left alone. She turns away from death toward life and, it appears, reaches to seize that life in Jesus. We can imagine her starting to throw her arms around him, perhaps even kiss him, in joy. But he says something curious to her, "Do not hold on to me, because I have not yet ascended to the Father" (Jn. 20:17). He sends her to tell the others that she has seen the Lord.

On one level Jesus is telling her not to touch him, as if perhaps he were in some intermediate stage of being that is neither corporeal nor incorporeal. He is there and yet not there for Mary, whereas for Thomas a week later he is shown to be wholly physical. What kind of body did the resurrected Christ have? It is not a question that needs to interest us much, even though the Church's creeds insist that he appeared in the body. What matters in Mary's encounter is not whether there is a body to hold on to. What Jesus is saying, I think, is more profound and more important. He says, "Don't cling to me." Jesus, even the resurrected Jesus, is not the point for Mary's life, nor for the lives of the disciples in community. Holding on to Jesus gets them nothing. That Jesus is raised from the dead and then ascends suggests that the Church has to let go of him in order to become what it needs to be. The Holy Spirit comes to be with us. Jesus goes.

Why, one might ask, resurrect him in the first place? Why not just send the Spirit? The risen Jesus is a mirror for our humanity and our divinity. In seeing him as she does, Mary sees her new self. In the same way, the disciples on the shore of the Sea of Tiberias see themselves in a new way when they are fed by the Risen One. The glory of God is revealed to them as an affirmation of abundant life in the face of suffering, chaos, death, fishless nights. But he is not the life so much as the sign of our deepest lives.

This third dimension of growth in the spirit is about recognizing this larger dimension of who we are and the profound nature of the *metanoia* that we are offered in eucharistic community. At this stage we begin to understand that the issue is not my personal salvation—my private elevation into God's presence. It is about our redemption as a people. The body of Christ was given for you—but not for you personally nor for me. It is for *us*, all of us. It is that change of heart that we are invited to know at breakfast with Jesus. It is what begins to make us adults.

Chapter 4

"Feed My Sheep"

15 When they had finished breakfast, Jesus said to Simon Peter, "Simon son of John, do you love me more than these?" He said to him, "Yes, Lord; you know that I love you." Jesus said to him, "Feed my lambs." 16 A second time he said to him, "Simon son of John, do you love me?" He said to him, "Yes, Lord; you know that I love you." Jesus said to him, "Tend my sheep." 17 He said to him the third time, "Simon son of John, do you love me?" Peter felt hurt because he said him the third time, "Do you love me?" And he said to him, "Lord, you know everything; you know that I love you." Jesus said to him, "Feed my sheep."

Breakfast is over. Now what? Jesus turns to Peter, who may be feeling sleepy after a long night and a good meal, and addresses him formally as Simon, son of John—not as Peter. It is not a good sign. "Do you love me more than these?" Perhaps without thinking, he replies, "Yes, Lord; you know that I love you." That was easy. Peter smiles. Jesus looks at him. All of the suppressed guilt returns, and in his head Peter sees the courtyard where he denied this man and all he stood for. What kind of love denies the beloved? The other disciples suddenly find things to do. There is a net full of fish to tend. They disappear, leaving Peter to confront Jesus on his own.

From our perspective as modern, educated people, it is impossible, I think, to put ourselves in this scene. Even those of us who are faithful, who profess to be Christians, must find it hard to imagine what it is like to be Peter seated on the sand next to Jesus, who was crucified and died. Who is it that asks, "Do you love me?" Is he alive, dead, a ghost, a figment? Does Jesus not know if Peter loves him? Or does he just want Peter to think about what it means to profess love for another person? What is the point of this conversation? Perhaps the more important question is not one based in historicizing this scene but one that asks: What does it mean for believers to profess love for Jesus the Christ?

A few years ago during Holy Week at St. Clement's Church, which was then my parish in New York, we created something we called the "Real Time Passion" in an effort to imagine what it was like to be with Jesus during the final hours of his life. We wanted to know what it meant to love Jesus at the time of his death by being with him. It was an effort to articulate love, to embody it, so that we could better understand it. The liturgical period of Holy Week is intended to bring to life Jesus' passion for believers. Since the fourth century, when Egeria the pilgrim witnessed and wrote about re-enactments of the Passion in Jerusalem,[1] the church has dramatized the events to a greater or lesser degree. Our enactment was

---

1. See Roger Greenacre and Jeremy Haselock, *The Sacrament of Easter* (Grand Rapids, MI: Wm B. Eerdmans Publishing Co., 1989), for a history of the development of the observance of Holy Week, including information on Egeria.

designed as a liturgy that took the place of our ordinary
lives for twenty-four hours.

Beginning with Maundy Thursday we followed the
story of Jesus' death from the Last Supper into the
Garden of Gethsemane to the courtyard outside the
Sanhedrin. We then witnessed his trial before Pilate
and walked the stations of the cross back to our church,
where we participated in the traditional three-hour
meditation on the cross. At sundown on Good Friday,
we entombed him in the tabernacle on the altar. We
were awake for twenty-four straight hours wandering
in the dark from church to church in lower Manhattan. Gethsemane was a simple garden attached to a
church in Chelsea. Peter denied Jesus in the courtyard
of a parish in Greenwich Village. We tried Jesus on the
steps of the chapel at The General Theological Seminary. We processed with the cross through midtown
Manhattan and Times Square, stopping to pray at "stations" such as Show World's Adult Emporium and the
site of a brutal murder.

Perhaps the most emotionally arresting moment of
the long journey to the cross is Peter's denial of Jesus.
At least it was for us on that night. We gathered
together in the courtyard of the church in Greenwich
Village and built a fire in a hibachi on a stone patio
table. We were cold. Between 2:00 in the morning and
dawn, we argued about whether Jesus deserved to die;
we confronted our own complicity in injustice. Some
of us were there as provocateurs, arguing the case
against him. But after denying Jesus three times, Bill,
the man portraying Peter, gave a moving, extempora-
neous speech in which he reflected on what he was feeling as an actor and as Peter. He gave us an insight into
his own spirit, where he was struggling with the

woundedness of his own fear and the denials that marked his life. We felt Peter's anguish in a new way through Bill's honesty. It was no longer possible to judge Peter as one who had failed. We had to be with him as we were with Bill: as one who is just like the rest of us.

It was a moving moment in which the idea behind the Real Time Passion was most clearly realized. The human Peter was revealed in the actor, equally human and known to all of us in his flawed humanity, as was the grace by which both of them were offered something more than their worst selves. The suffering of Peter's separation (and this actor's coming to terms with his own separation from others) was a sign of Jesus' distance from us and from those who were with him when he was alive. In the scene as we enacted it the man portraying Jesus was never visible. He was somewhere else, being interrogated. We did not see him again until Pilate presented him to the crowd several hours later. During the long night, Jesus was isolated and so was Peter. We all can understand this experience of being separated from those we love or from the source of our strength, whatever that might be. As I discussed in chapter one, isolation is a condition to which we frequently return in our lives and from which we long to escape. Around the fire in that courtyard, Peter descended into the deepest isolation imaginable, made worse by his own actions in shutting himself off from the one person who most deeply loved him—and whom he most deeply loved.

This moment after breakfast by the lake is surely meant to recall that moment of isolation in the courtyard. It is all the more poignant because of that recollection of the three-fold denial, which is reinforced by the thrice-repeated question, "Do you love me?" Jesus does not question Peter's response. He does not reply, as most of us might, "Then why did you deny me?" He simply says, "Feed my sheep."

For Peter, at this moment, it might seem that Jesus has come back from the dead for this reason only, to ridicule him, to accuse him by his repeated question, and then to give him an absurd instruction. Peter, like us, does not welcome judgment. It is not the way we prefer to be with Jesus. When we encounter him in eucharist and in Scripture, as we know we can, we expect comfort and hope. But the truth is that the resurrection also questions us. In it we are challenged, if we are paying attention, to be honest about who we are. It is a call to authenticity, and that can sometimes feel like judgment. We need to have the kind of dialogue with him that Peter has in this passage. It is essential that we meet the risen Jesus with this kind of clarity if we are to grow in our faith. As people who have denied Jesus and our own identities, we need to confront our denials to awaken our vocation as Christians. It is the next stage on our journey toward spiritual wisdom.

The gospel writer notes that this is the third time the risen Jesus has appeared to the disciples. Jesus keeps coming back. The resurrection happens for each of us as an awakening to faith. In the Gospel of John he reappears through the power of the Holy Spirit, the Paraclete, who shows us in Scripture the way to truth. The Scripture itself is a resurrection appearance. It is in that sense that I first read John 21 as a call for my own life— not in seeing the physical Jesus but in knowing the Spirit, the Comforter, on the banks of the Hudson through the vehicle of Scripture.

I began this chapter by asking what it might have been like to be Peter in that moment with Jesus after breakfast, but not because I think of it as a moment in real time. The point is not whether this conversation with Peter actually happened and what it might have been like for the historical Peter. The passage is meaningful as a story in itself—stories are a primary way in which we come to know God—but if we do not read the story in terms of our own lives, it loses its power to change us. The Scripture is not a magic wand. We have to "eat" the word, as Ezekiel does when Yahweh charges him to speak to Israel (Ez. 3:3); we need to have this dialogue with Jesus ourselves. We need to hear for our own lives what Jesus says to Peter: "Feed my sheep." What is the meaning of this question for each of us?

One way to phrase it is: Do what you are. Now this is not the same thing as the situation I described in chapter one in which we define ourselves entirely—our very essence—by our work: you are what you do. Jesus is not offering Peter a job description. What he is saying is: do what you are—for others. That is the real message here. If you love me, you will feed my sheep. You will take care of those who need to be cared for. That is your vocation, however it is realized in the world.

Jesus asks Peter this question three times, and Peter affirms three times his love for Jesus. And three times Jesus tells him what to do to make that love real. Peter is hurt, as you and I would be, because the repetition suggests that Peter does not get the message. He might wonder if Jesus isn't rubbing salt in the wound.

"Yes, Lord," he says, "you know that I love you." All right! I get it!

Now Peter can get it. In this model of spiritual life that we have been tracking, Peter has come by way of evolving spiritual practice through *metanoia* to a dimension of new possibilities. Most importantly, once he is reconciled to God he can live his Christian vocation in the world. That is the essential commandment—not to convert the world, but to reconcile the world to God. This work begins at home. When Jesus and Peter are reconciled, Peter is to go and do likewise. The divine seeks us in resurrection, that act of reconciliation in which we are promised that nothing can permanently alienate us from God's love. As Paul writes, God "reconciled us to himself through Christ, and has given us the ministry of reconciliation" (2 Cor.5:18b).

Reconciliation is hard work, however, as Peter's hurt suggests. At the heart of our uneasiness with the work of reconciliation is our vulnerability to others—to their wrath, their ridicule, their rejection. Suppose I ask if you love me and you say that you don't. Then what? Suppose I ask your forgiveness and you refuse me? How do I make it clear to you that I want reconciliation? Before we can be reconciled to others we have to be reconciled to ourselves. Otherwise our uncertainty about who we are interferes with our encounter with others. Our vulnerability blocks openness. Peter is troubled by his past, a relationship with Jesus that has not always been smooth. Even though he is regarded as the spokesman for the disciples, and in this chapter of John as spokesman for the church, his hurt signals that he lacks self-confidence. His wounds have not healed—and until they do he cannot help others be reconciled to God and to themselves. Although Peter does not yet realize it, his wounds—the very fact of having denied Jesus—are a source of his own healing.

Peter is a well-known and beloved figure in the New Testament. He emerges as a model Christian leader, the emblem of apostleship that we can identify with because he is so human and at the same time larger than life. No New Testament character is more fully drawn than Peter. Throughout John's gospel, however, he is always at odds with the Beloved Disciple—and by telling Peter to feed his sheep, the gospel writer (through Jesus) seems to be instructing both Peter and his community on appropriate modes of discipleship. In this reading, Peter is not a hero, not the ideal disciple, but rather a flawed leader who needs to be corrected. He is an example of Henri Nouwen's wounded healer. In forcing Peter to look closely at what it means—what it might mean—for him to love him, Jesus calls him to a deeper understanding of his own pain, and (borrowing Nouwen's words)

> makes it possible for him to convert his weakness into strength and to offer his own experience as a source of healing to those who are often lost in the darkness of their own misunderstood sufferings. . . . Making one's own wounds a source of healing, therefore, does not call for a sharing of superficial personal pains but for a constant willingness to see one's own pain and suffering as rising from the depth of the human condition which all share.[2]

In confronting Peter in this way, Jesus reminds him that he is mortal and, at the same time, leads him to understand that his condition is a source of liberation, for himself and for others. It is out of this understanding that reconciliation is possible. As Nouwen

---

2. Henri Nouwen, *The Wounded Healer* (New York: Doubleday Image Books, 1979), pp. 87, 88.

says of the wounded healer as minister, "the wound, which causes us to suffer now, will be revealed to us later as the place where God intimated his new creation."[3] Jesus reveals Peter's vocation to him. It is our vocation as well, the vocation of all Christians, both as individuals and as part of the institution of the church.

This dialogue that Jesus initiates with Peter seems to come out of nowhere. Until now, John 21 has been a fishing story that is also about the formation of community through a common meal. It has seemed to be an endorsement of Peter's evolving leadership in the church. He is the one who has made all of the decisions and taken the important actions. Suddenly, however, Jesus is not only putting Peter on the spot, he is talking about sheep not fish. Although these sheep might appear to be a detour, they are important to the idea of vocation as a dimension of spiritual growth. Who are these sheep? Perhaps more importantly: Who are the shepherds? As one commentator has observed, the shift from fish and water to sheep and wilderness is not a change of subject so much as a change of key. Fish is to water as sheep is to wilderness, and both are potent images for Israel and the early church.[4]

In the book of Genesis, Abel was a keeper of sheep and Jacob cared for his own flock. In the book of the prophet Ezekiel, written soon after the final editing of Genesis, God is pictured as one who seeks out the scattered sheep, the people of Israel in exile (Ezek. 34:11-30).

3. Ibid., p. 96.
4. Edmund Leach, "Fishing for Men on the Edge of the Wilderness," in Robert Alter and Frank Kermode, eds., *The Literary Guide to the Bible* (Cambridge, MA: Belknap Press, Harvard University Press, 1987), pp. 592-93. Leach's article pointed me to a number of interesting parallels between John 21 and the Hebrew Scriptures and offered suggestive insights inot the relationship between Exodus and the feeding of the multitudes.

The image of the shepherd is also one that stood for national leaders ruling over their people; it was common in Mesopotamia and Egypt, as well as in Israel. The shepherd leading his sheep is a favorite symbol for depicting the Exodus, as in the Song of Moses, where God is implicitly present as a shepherd leading the people to safe pasture. This image becomes explicit in Psalm 78:

> Then he led out his people like sheep,
> and guided them in the wilderness like a flock.
> He led them in safety, so that they were not afraid;
> but the sea overwhelmed their enemies.
> And he brought them to his holy hill,
> to the mountain that his right hand had won.
> (Ps. 78:52-54).

Even here, the sea is not too far behind. The twenty-third psalm is the classic expression of this imagery: "The Lord is my shepherd, I shall not want."

For the purposes of this conversation between Peter and Jesus, the political implications of the shepherd motif are particularly important. The good king is a good shepherd (as David the shepherd became the quintessential king for Israel). But Ezekiel uses the image of the bad shepherd to identify the characteristics of selfish and irresponsible leadership (34:2-3):

> Thus says the Lord God: Ah, you shepherds of Israel who have been feeding yourselves! Should not shepherds feed the sheep? You eat the fat, you clothe yourselves with the wool, you slaughter the fatlings; but you do not feed the sheep.[5]

---

5. Ezekiel was active at the time of the fall of Jerusalem to the Babylonians in 586, a collapse he attributes to the faithlessness of King Zedekiah. See Raymond E. Brown et. al., *The New Jerome Biblical Commentary*, "Ezekiel" (Englewood Cliffs, NJ: Prentice Hall, 1990), p. 306.

This imagery is also important in John's Gospel, where Jesus' genuine care for Israel is contrasted with the faithlessness of the temple leadership. The author of John has specifically identified the mission and death of Jesus with his role as a shepherd by using ideas from Ezekiel 34 ("I myself will be the shepherd of my sheep."), as well as Zechariah 13:7: "Strike the shepherd, that the sheep may be scattered." Zechariah was especially significant for the early disciples and their understanding of Jesus' eschatological program. Both of these passages have a powerful impact on the use of this imagery in the gospels and, indeed, on the church's interpretation of the death and resurrection of Jesus. So the dialogue between Peter and Jesus in this chapter of John would have resonated deeply with its hearers.

Jesus' threefold questioning of Peter is more than just a literary or theological reversal of Peter's triple denial in the courtyard before Jesus' death, although it is that. The recollection of Peter's denial also has psychological importance, as we have seen. But these passages from Ezekiel and Zechariah—both prophets attacking the shepherds who do not properly care for the sheep—indicate the importance of this encounter between Jesus and Peter. Ultimately, John's message is about the church in the first century, and for the church in the modern era, and how each cares for the sheep of its pasture. For the early church, Jesus is the good shepherd who lays down his life for the sheep in contrast to the faithless shepherds. In Zechariah, however, there is a different shepherd, a messianic figure whom the church later identifies with the stricken Christ:[6]

---

6. These oracles in Zechariah 9-14 are less concerned with historical circumstances than they are with eschatology. See ibid., p. 353.

"Awake, O sword, against my shepherd,
against the man who is my associate,"
says the Lord of hosts.
Strike the shepherd, that the sheep may be
scattered (13:7).

Peter is one who has assisted in "striking the shepherd" by denying Jesus and now has to face the stricken one, who asks him to become one of the good shepherds, one of those who feed the sheep and not themselves. If Peter is the head of the church and the leader of the apostles, why does Jesus need to instruct him in this way? Peter knows what the shepherd is to do. He has heard what Ezekiel and Zechariah have to say on the subject.

The message to Peter and to church leaders everywhere is simply this: your job is not to run an institution, it is to take care of people's needs. The author of this chapter of John represents a community that has sought to form itself as a community of love, not one of institutional power. The implicit warning to Peter here, and in the subsequent sections of this chapter, is that he cannot manage the kingdom without caring for the sheep. The sheep in fact are the kingdom. They are what matter. The shepherd charged with their care is responsible to God and to no one else—and will be judged by God alone. Even church leaders can become worthless shepherds.

Thus Peter is hurt by Jesus' suggestion that he is not a good shepherd, that his conception of vocation is flawed. His personal feelings are not the point; he needs to stop feeling sorry for himself and get on with the work that he has been given. The warning here is prophetic: I love you, says the Lord your God, but after awhile I will strike you down if you do not take care of those who cannot care for themselves. As Jesus says in Matthew 25, when he describes the separation of the sheep from the goats according to how they treated the hungry, the thirsty, the alien, the naked, the sick, and the imprisoned: "just as you did it to one of the least of these who are members of my family, you did it to me" (Matt. 25:40). If you love me, Jesus says to Peter, you will feed my sheep.

Attending church once a week has become for many of us the equivalent of having a spiritual life. While it is true that the spiritual life includes what we do—and is meaningless if we do nothing—the quality of our actions is also important. Going to church is not a leisure activity, like watching football on television, nor even a beneficial activity, like exercising. It should not be an activity at all but rather a practice, undertaken intentionally as part of a larger process of spiritual endeavor designed to change or reorient our lives. If we go to church for the same reason we go to the gym to work out—to develop the spiritual equivalent of buns of steel—we have not embraced the vocation of being Christian. A good workout is useful but it is only for my benefit. It has nothing to do with anyone else.

The journey toward spiritual wisdom is about learning and practicing the vocation of being Christian. Part of the essential work of this journey is to become reconciled to ourselves and to others. The image of this reconciliation is the Sabbath as it is practiced in Judaism but that is mostly lost to Christianity. Sabbath requires full-time vocation even though it is only one day a week. It is not about going to *shul*; rather, it is a condition of reconciliation in which we find rest (in

Hebrew *manuha*) that is more than just a ceasing of labor. Sabbath is a sign of our spiritual vocation. Abraham Joshua Heschel writes:

> To the biblical mind *menuha* is the same as happiness and stillness, as peace and harmony. The word with which Job described the state after life he was longing for is derived from the same root as *menuha*. It is the state wherein man lies still, wherein the wicked cease from troubling and the weary are at rest. It is the state in which there is no strife and no fighting, no fear and no distrust. The essence of the good life is *menuha*. "The Lord is my shepherd, I shall not want, He maketh me to lie down in green pastures; He leadeth me beside the still waters" (the waters of *menuhot*). In later times *menuha* became a synonym for the life in the world to come, for eternal life.[7]

Peter and Jesus have their conversation beside the still waters of the Sea of Galilee, where the sheep have been fed by the good shepherd and shown how they too are to feed the sheep. This breakfast by the lake is both eucharist and Sabbath: it is the moment when one's life and vocation are one.

As we learn in the eucharist, where the stranger is revealed as our true selves, our vocations are not our own. We grow in relationship with others—one might say we have no identity without others. This relatedness requires constant attention. The dialogue between Peter and Jesus is a painful reminder of the call to the hard work of love and commitment, not only in our private lives but in our social obligations. We are not

---

7. Abraham Joshua Heschel, *The Sabbath* (New York: Farrar, Straus and Giroux, 1951, 1979), p. 23.

allowed to answer Jesus' question just once. After the
hungry are fed, they get hungry again. We have to go
back to the Christ in our prayer and practice again and
again, just as we return to the eucharist repeatedly. The
dimensions of our life in faith overlap. We are never
fully enlightened; we can never get this right once and
for all. We are not expected to. We are not reconciled
by our own efforts but rather through the grace of God.
This dialogue between Peter and Jesus is about that
freely given grace. Not only is Peter reconciled to God
in Jesus' death and resurrection—as we all are—but
Peter is given the grace, as we are, of doing God's work
according to God's will and not his own. Some of us
have seen this as ordination. Others have seen it as
faithful living in the world. My particular form of calling is to be in both places as a deacon—both in the
church and in the world, reconciling one to the other
through the sign of my own daily living. It is not easy.

It is easy for most of us to understand ordained
ministry as a form of Christian vocation. It is harder
to see other kinds of work as an expression of Christian vocation. For most of my life, I have been a communications professional. I was an editor and publisher
of books for twenty-five years. For ten years I was a
consultant in electronic and print media and, for three
years, an editor of an interreligious journal. In a parallel life, I have written and published poetry, written
plays that were produced professionally, and written
books on spirituality. Along with these lives, I have
been a husband and father, raising two children. I am
a deacon who also leads retreats.

Is there one vocation in this life of many parallel
tracks? Some might even wonder if there is one person leading these lives. The truth is that it has taken

me this long to begin to understand how it all fits together, how these pieces are all part of a spiritual journey and not a career. As a professional in communications, I feed the sheep, especially as I have come to appreciate that what I do is for others. My work changes people's lives and contributes to the enrichment of the world. Books that I have edited and published have made a difference; articles I have published have contributed directly to the growth of interfaith relations; I hope that what I write has instructed or inspired people. One might even call this work diaconal in the deepest sense because it has been performed most often in the service of others.

All work can reflect these deeper values of service. That perspective on daily life grows, however, from an appreciation of vocation as I am using the term here. Embarking on a spiritual path such as Christianity changes who we are and therefore makes what we do into something more than a way to make a living. Some editors think of their work as a dimension of spiritual practice. Most do not. The same can be said of financial planners or travel agents.

In this fourth dimension of spiritual life, as new creations in Christ, as people who have changed, we do not leave our previous lives behind. They are still part of us, as Peter's denial is always a part of who he is (just as it would be for us). There is no Peter who did not deny Jesus. After ordination, I remained the same old flawed fellow I was before. I remained an editor and writer. I was made a deacon by the Holy Spirit, but I am still Ken. As Ken I am in constant dialogue with the people in my life whom I have loved and hurt, and also with those whose articles I publish or whose web sites I help to bring into existence. I have to work at

integrating these aspects of my identity with my sense
of vocation. Who am I in the world? Who are you in
the world? This is a question not only of what you do.
But it includes what you do and how you do it. This
dialogue with Jesus is one we are called to have constantly with the divine that resides within us.

I tried, on one occasion, to enter this conversation,
to become part of the story either as Peter or Jesus. I
sat on a bench in a grove at a retreat center on a cool
and soft afternoon. Around me were statues, probably
of Mary and Francis, although I do not remember
exactly. But I had had such extraordinary experiences
with this technique of discernment, I wanted to step
into this dialogue and determine whether I was called
by God to ordained ministry.

I closed my eyes and tried to see myself by the
lake, following breakfast, perhaps seated on the sand
by the dying fire. The other disciples had disappeared. They were not important to the story, which
after all was only about Jesus and me and my vocation. I wanted a one-on-one. Nothing else would do.
But I felt, for the first time, nothing but emptiness.
There was literally no one there to speak with me. I
tried to conjure Jesus. I probably even opened my
eyes slightly and stared at one of the plaster statues
to animate it. Nothing. And then I felt the dread of
being abandoned. For a long time I sat with the
emptiness and experienced it as fear. God had left me.
The one who had so cheerfully attended when I
called was gone. My fellow actor in these exercises
had disappeared.

After awhile, I got up and walked across the long
lawn in front of the retreat center toward the far side
of the property, hoping that in my walk I might find

some company. I had not yet learned, as I was to discover much later in my life, how to sit with emptiness and understand it not as abandonment but as the purest presence. Presence for me then was only to be found in something that looked and sounded human and was there exclusively for me. I was like the disciples in that sense: they needed that encounter with the Risen Jesus on the shore to restore their sense of his having been with them at all. It was not enough to remember, to know that he was once there. They needed that reassurance of love.

Jesus does not need Peter's reassurance of love beside the sea. He asks if Peter loves him to remind Peter of the consequences of Jesus' having loved him first.

I walked for awhile and knew nothing more than I had when I started. A wind sprang up and I began to feel chilly. I turned back toward the retreat house and, in effect, stopped thinking about anything at all. I was simply the walk. At some point, I realized that someone was coming toward me, someone I did not recognize. This figure was clothed in a robe of some sort and looked just barely corporeal. I could see through him, in fact. His facial features were indistinct. As he approached, he opened his arms to embrace me. I stepped into the embrace and for a moment *felt* something there. Then I was alone again.

It was the dialogue I had sought, only turned toward what I needed more than anything else at that point in my life: the assurance of God's love for me. It turned out that I did not need to enter into a dialogue about love and responsibility, or life and calling. God meets us where we are, as in this chapter from John, Jesus meets Peter where he is and as he is.

How do we practice this presence of God? How do we open ourselves to it? In it we offer ourselves as we are to God, and God offers to us the presence of the Spirit. One way in which we make ourselves available is by entering the stillness of *menuha*, the Sabbath rest, the time of blessing following the common meal. It is a form of prayer, meditation, that brings us back constantly to the presence of God. (Jesus keeps asking Peter, "Do you love me?" I imagine that Peter went on hearing this question all of his life. Perhaps we should be hearing it constantly too.) Even though God is always with us (*we* do not make God present), we need to be actively aware of that presence and to be actively engaged in the work of reconciliation that presence requires of us. We need to go for the walk that allows us to encounter the one who is also out walking—or we need to go fishing so that the One who knows the fish can show us where we need to be.

The Risen One offers assurance of divine presence. Christ keeps coming back. And his faithfulness is a call to us to be risen as well. Just as we are buried with Christ in baptism—just as Peter is buried in the Lake in his baptism—so are we raised with him in his resurrection. Peter too is raised, in this chapter of John, with Christ. We are called constantly to awaken.

What is our vocation as Christians? It is the vocation of all faithful people—to be present, to bear witness to the joy that is within us. Once we know what our vocation is, we can feed God's sheep. We can do that individual work we are called to do. Too often we confuse vocation with ordination or some kind of separate holy calling. In fact, we all have the same vocation; what is different is how we each carry it out in the world. The dimension of spiritual life we are

describing here is the understanding of that fundamental vocation, which is in relation to the risen Christ
who makes it possible to be reconciled and to reconcile. At the heart of our conflicts within the church
these days is a failure to recognize in each other this
shared vocation. My vocation is who I am.

Failure to understand the nature of this vocation is
also at the heart of our isolation in a culture that does
not understand or appreciate or honor the notion of
bearing witness that Christianity requires. In isolation,
we cannot be a witness to anyone or anything. If our
primary concern is whether God will take care of and
enrich me, then we are unlikely to be able to witness
to anyone but our own egos. A best-selling book enti-
tled *The Prayer of Jabez: Breaking Through to the Blessed
Life*[8] contains a prayer uttered by an otherwise
unknown figure in 1 Chronicles 4:10 called Jabez:

> And Jabez called on the God of Israel saying,
> "Oh, that You would bless me indeed
> and enlarge my territory,
> and that your hand might be with me,
> and that You would keep me from evil,
> that I may not cause pain!"
> So God granted him what he requested.

This little book was a bestseller because it promises
that, by saying the right words—*this* prayer—each of
us will gain favor with God and our lives will be
enriched. Material blessings will be ours. What is
wrong with this version of Christian faith? The author's
motivation is clearly to help people, but what comes

---

8. Bruce Wilkinson, *The Prayer of Jabez: Breaking Through to the Blessed Life*
(Sisters, OR: Multnomah Publishers, 2000)

through is a vision of faith in which God plays favorites and distributes rewards to those who ask for them in faith, but *withholds* blessings from others. *The Prayer of Jabez* tells a parable of a man who goes to heaven and finds in a large warehouse a box full of blessings that he did not receive from God because he failed to ask for them. Blessing depends on a system of exchange. Jesus, however, says nothing to Peter of the rewards he can expect for living in faithful love. Instead, he asks that Peter practice love for others because that is his vocation, not in order to receive blessings for his good works.

The next section of John 21, which I will discuss in Chapter Five, is even more explicit about the consequences of the way of life to which Peter and all Christians are called. The way of faithful living—or the path of wisdom—that this chapter of John advocates is not one that has gained a large following. The earliest Christians began by walking this way and then, as the church became a powerful institution, fewer of them remembered what it was like to follow Jesus on the way. The church too has a vocation, as we do. The author of John has a different vision of the church's vocation. He warns that the church will lose its soul and its very reason for being if it forgets the prophecies of Ezekiel and Zechariah, if it forgets that the death of Jesus was the result of evil done by bad shepherds. When my friends at St. Clement's and I attempted to walk the way of Jesus' passion in order to find the way of Jesus' wisdom, the impulse was not in itself wrong. We tried to "put on" Jesus in order to feel what it might have been like to be him. But in fact we know what it is like to be him. We live exactly as he did in the grip of time and space, and we feel what he felt. In fact, we are not called to live his life but ours, only more fully because of what he shows us about ourselves. In time we will feel everything that he felt because we will die, as he died—perhaps not as brutally or as the victim of injustice. But around us every day are those who die in just that way, brutally and as victims. We know exactly what that is like. As Christians when we fail to take care of those who die brutally, or those who cannot eat or have no place to live or are tortured for their beliefs, we are saying "No" in answer to Jesus' question "Do you love me?" We are denying him exactly as Peter did in that courtyard. The profound failure of Christianity—in its personal and institutional forms—is manifest in those who starve in every country of the world and in the profound indifference of western society to the impact of our way of life on the world's ability to support any life.

Peter is ashamed of what he has been. So am I, quite often, ashamed of my failures and the church's failures in the practice of our vocation. Shame does not take us anywhere, however. I have discovered that it is important for Jesus and me to have this conversation all the time. It is not a one-time quiz. We have to keep working at the issue: How is God's love made manifest in my life? How is my vocation to be a witness to the presence of God expressed in faithfulness?

Chapter 5

"Others Will Tie You Up"

18 "Very truly, I tell you, when you were younger, you used to fasten your own belt and to go wherever you wished. But when you grow old, you will stretch out your hands, and someone else will fasten a belt around you and take you where you do not wish to go."19 (He said this to indicate the kind of death by which he would glorify God.) After this he said to him, "Follow me."

As an angler I do not kill many fish. When I do they are usually salt-water, mostly bluefish, which are plentiful. It is rare for me to kill a trout, and when I catch one, I release it as quickly as possible to avoid causing it too much stress. But there is no question that the event of being caught and hauled out of the water is traumatic for a fish, even when it is allowed to live. We imagine ourselves to be like trout, freely swimming creatures who go where we wish to go. If we are clever, we can avoid the angler stalking us from the shore.

Once on the Wood River in Rhode Island I caught and killed a trout when my son and I were canoeing. It was, I think, a shock to him to watch me do it. He was twelve at the time and had been fishing with me on a couple of previous occasions, when I released every fish. The canoe trip was an annual event for the two of us, occurring during the two- or three-week period we spent each summer at the family cottage on the shore. The Wood is a lovely stream that, in its upper reaches in what is known as the Acadia Management Area, is slow-flowing and cedar-colored. It is not very deep, although it has some surprising holes that contain large trout.

On this day, we were catching no fish, except for salmon fry—the fingerlings planted in the river by some optimistic fishery planners who hoped to reinstitute an annual salmon run from the Atlantic upriver to old and long abandoned spawning grounds. The salmon snapped annoyingly at everything that moved. None were more than three or four inches in length. As we paddled down stream we kept our eyes open for trout feeding on the surface. They would be the easiest to catch from the canoe. When we came to a sweeping bend in the river, we heard a loud splash just out of sight beyond the jut of land to our right. I propelled the canoe into the open and saw, beneath an overhanging bush, the ripples from the rise of what had to be a large fish. I beached the canoe on the left side of the bend and, still kneeling in it, flicked what is known as a hare's ear nymph onto the surface of the stream, just about ten feet above the point where the fish was feeding.

A hare's ear nymph is not intended to imitate any particular insect. It just looks buggy. Bounced along the bottom of a stream, it might be a May fly in its nymph or larval stage. Floated on the surface, as I was using it on this particular day, a hare's ear could be almost anything good to eat. The artificial fly drifted over the epicenter of the ring of dying ripples. Bursting into the air and rising several inches above the surface, a sub-stantial brown trout snatched the fly and fell with a splash into the water. I tightened the line; he was hooked. He may have been too surprised to fight very hard because within a couple of minutes I had the fish on the small bank in front of the canoe. The trout was impressive—approximately twenty inches in length, weighing about five pounds. Deeply colored and strong, it gave me a hard look with its one exposed eye.

Nick asked me, "What are you going to do, dad?"

"Kill it," I said, pulling out my Swiss Army knife.

His eyes grew round. I quickly slit the trout's throat. It flapped a couple of times and then lay still. I cut a ventral slit from throat to anal opening, exposing the internal organs. By now, my hands were shaking and covered with blood. Nick sat back to watch. I reached my hand inside the body cavity and scooped out the guts, tossing them into the river. It was a serious, pri-mal moment, and I felt the power of killing sweep through my body. Nick could see it in my face.

"What's wrong," he asked.

"Nothing," I said, washing the gutted fish in the river.

"Are we going to eat it?"

"We're not killing it for fun."

Death comes to us just as it did to that brown trout. One moment we are safe, eating dinner with family or friends, and the next we are gone. A curmudgeonly but beloved musician at St. Clement's was hiking in the woods the day after his sixty-second birthday when he simply fell to his knees and then on his face and died. There was no warning. He may not have known that he was dying. Every one of us will go in just this way, without knowing ahead of time exactly when or how. Crossing a street, talking animatedly with a friend, we may not see the taxi that makes a quick turn into us. Some of us have a clearer vision of the end than others. If we are in the hospital about to undergo heart surgery, we may suspect that death is waiting in the operating room. I remember visiting a woman the evening before she was to have open-heart surgery and being struck by how frightened she was. I tried to reassure her, but she knew she was going to die. And she did.

Everyone dies, and one way to hear what Jesus says to Peter is simply that: you will die as I died. When we are young we believe that we will live forever and that we can do whatever we want to do. The young believe in immortality. There are no limits to the youthful imagination. It is only as we age that we begin to understand how our options have changed. If I want to be a mathematician or tennis player, I should be performing at near peak capacity by my mid-twenties. At fifty-seven, it is too late for me to take up a career in professional sports. The poet I wanted to be in my twenties became a publisher. I will not go backpacking around Europe or cross the Pacific on a tramp steamer. It was always possible that I could drop dead at any moment. And the longer I live the more likely it is that I will drop dead tomorrow. It is only as I have aged that I have come to understand that as a reality, an eventuality, not a mere and distant chance. I will lose my life.

The third time Jesus asks, "Simon son of John, do you love me?" Peter is understandably hurt. Jesus replies, "Feed my sheep"—and almost callously goes on, without a pause, to make what seems in the context this odd prediction. "But when you grow old, you will stretch out your hands, and someone else will fasten a belt around you and take you where you do not wish to go." What does the one have to do with the other? Is Jesus saying, "If you do what I am asking, you will lose your freedom, your sense of self, control over your very body"? Here the invitation to follow Jesus is clearly an invitation to loss of self, even to death. The "Follow me" at the conclusion of this section is not simply an invitation to be a disciple or a student. It is an invitation to follow the way of Jesus in all of its radical dimensions, including death and resurrection.

Jesus does speak to Peter about what the writer describes as "the kind of death he was to die," using the same language in which, earlier in the gospel, he alludes to his own death: "'And I, when I am lifted up from the earth, will draw all people to myself.' He said this to indicate the kind of death he was to die" (12:32-33). One implication is that Peter will also be martyred—and, in fact, by the time this chapter of John was written, Peter had been martyred in Rome. His martyrdom is less important for us than the limiting of his spiritual options. This apparent narrowing of choices should not be viewed negatively, however, because it frees Peter to be more deeply himself—and us to become more deeply ourselves, if we live with our eyes open. As our circumstances narrow, our senses become keener. We become like the blind who develop a stronger sense of smell and touch. We become more acutely aware of the urgency and at the same time the serenity of our lives. We do not want to squander what we have, and at the same time what we have is more than sufficient for our purposes.

In the Acts of Peter, an early Christian text that did not become part of the New Testament, there is a scene that reiterates how difficult it is for Peter, and for us, to accept the reality that is our lives. According to this story, Peter is being hunted by certain husbands in Rome who blame his preaching for their wives' suddenly embracing chastity. Xanthippe, the wife of Agrippa, warns Peter that her husband intends to have him executed. His fellow Christians also urge him to escape Rome in order to serve the Lord (being more useful alive than dead). Convinced that he should go, and once again evading the consequences of his life choices, Peter escapes the city in disguise. The story continues:

> And as he went out of the gate, he saw the Lord entering Rome; and when he saw him he said, "Lord, where are you going?" And the Lord said to him, "I am coming to Rome to be crucified." And Peter said unto him, "Lord, are you being crucified again?" He said to him, "Yes, Peter, I am being crucified again." And Peter came to himself; and he saw the Lord ascending into Heaven; then he returned to Rome, rejoicing and giving praise to the Lord, because he said, "I am being crucified"; since this was to happen to Peter.[1]

And, according to legend, Peter was captured and crucified—upside down, so as not to claim equality with Jesus in death.

1. Willis Barnstone, ed., *The Acts of Peter*, in *The Other Bible* (New York: HarperSanFrancisco, 1984), p. 442.

One of the critical questions for Peter's life is, when will he follow Jesus? When will Peter give his life fully to Christ and become most completely himself? In Matthew, Mark, and Luke Peter is called from his fishing nets at the beginning of Jesus' ministry and instantly responds by leaving his work to follow Jesus. He gives up everything, without a second thought, and goes with Jesus. The story is not so simple in John. Jesus does not call Peter from his fishing. Instead, we read:

> Simon Peter said to him, "Lord, where are you going?" Jesus answered, "Where I am going, you cannot follow me now; but you will follow afterward." Peter said to him, "Lord, why can I not follow you now? I will lay down my life for you." Jesus answered, "Will you lay down your life for me? Very truly, I tell you, before the cock crows, you will have denied me three times" (John 13:36-38).

In this gospel Peter does not drop everything to follow Jesus, even though he believes that he would. He does deny Jesus, as everyone knows, and the church clearly remembers, in such accounts as the Acts of Peter, that he was not at all the perfectly obedient follower.

In John's Gospel Jesus does not ask Peter to follow him until the final chapter, when at this reminder of Peter's certain death, Jesus says, "Follow me." It does not matter whether Jesus asks Peter to follow him at the beginning or at the end of his ministry. In both accounts, Jesus calls him from the work that defines him by what he does to work that defines him according to who he is. The result is the same. Peter's life options are narrowed by the vocation Jesus calls him to embrace—and at the same time he is freed to be recreated in the image of God. He is a mirror image, to be sure: he is nailed on an inverted cross.

Like Jesus, however, he gives up his life for the sheep he has been given, however reluctantly. In asking Peter to follow him—or in asking us to follow him—is Jesus merely inviting us to death? Does this invitation offer an option, a choice?

In workshops on dying, a common exercise is to imagine what you would do if you had only a year to live. Usually, people say they would take the trip they have been putting off or reconcile with estranged relatives or take the time to appreciate the natural world they have neglected for their work. The point of the workshop is simply that since you cannot know when you will die, you should act now as if you had only a year or even less to live. Death is a present not a distant reality. Our ability to know that makes us both human and spiritual beings.

The life of the spirit is also about death, a dying to self that makes this fifth dimension of spiritual life hard for us. After I have spent my life trying to understand who I am and what I want, now I have to give it up? Jesus says that we do not choose our own destination, and we resist that spiritual reality as much as we resist death. We want to believe that we are in charge of our own lives. We resist the notion that we are asked, as the rich young ruler was asked, to sell all that we have—to give away whatever it is we consider essential to our identities in order to become ourselves. Our encounter with Christ will change us and send us where we do not expect or even want to go. When we lose control of our own destinies in this way, we call it being set free in Christ without knowing perhaps what

that means. Our essential vocation is to bear witness.
That is a radical, ego-threatening state of awareness, a
state in which people can get killed. But to learn that
who we most deeply are is not the ego we prize is a
profound gift of freedom, not a limitation. It is the only
way to die as a free person.

One might argue persuasively that choice itself
has become the dominant religion of the West. It
does not matter what we choose or what the choices
are—all that is important is that we *can* choose. This
is the essence of the consumer mentality, that there
are forty brands of cereal to choose among or fifty
churches. All of them have fiber and sugar; some
have raisins. The Internet is the perfect icon of contemporary life. It is fundamentally about choice,
nothing but the endless proliferation of options, any
one of which is as good as another. The choices are
also randomized, even when we go in search of a
particular object. Other objects always arrive unin-
vited. Those of us who "surf" the web are no longer
surprised when a search for "pants" turns up
unwanted pornographic links or when amazon.com
welcomes us by name and seems to know what kind
of book or CD we will want to buy. Even the most
benign web sites now carry banner advertising. The
world-wide web is the perfect advertising medium:
every object can be attached to a commercial message, which is extremely cheap to send to anyone
with a computer. Our life of endless choosing is in
fact a product of the consumer (or advertising) mentality in which everything is for sale. Left alone, we
might want nothing but food, shelter, and company.
Advertising shapes desire, as every marketer knows.
In the community of constant choice, desire is all

there is. Endless desire, as the ancient myth of Tantalus demonstrated, is the same as eternal suffering.

Religious experience and faith itself have been profoundly affected by this culture of choice. The biggest sellers are those that examine the marketing of religion. What are people buying? How are the successful religions positioning themselves? What packs in the crowds? It appears that syncretism works: pieces of any religion may be combined with parts of others to form endless private expressions of belief. For example, a person might practice Zen meditation as part of a holistic program of self-healing that includes Astanga Yoga and chants invoking Shiva and Shakti (male and female Hindu gods). This same person might attend services of the Unity Church, which is a somewhat gnostic and respectable version of Christianity, while invoking the aid of guardian angels. These arrangements can be altered at will, shifted as needed, abandoned when they become unwieldy or when something more interesting comes along. What many contemporary, especially young, people *don't* want is dogmatism. Some see this situation as a welcome culture of pluralism that frees us from religious and doctrinal tyranny; others embrace fundamentalist certainty in order to liberate themselves from the tyrannies of choice. Both options—a religion I construct for myself or one that is "ready to wear"—seem to be primarily about personal satisfaction. They supply answers and are intended to comfort. Paradox and doubt have no place in either the culture of unlimited choice or the realm of unquestioned assurance because they provide no answers and cause discomfort. What good is religion, one might say, if it does not tell me a transparent truth about the universe—and most importantly my place in it? Eclecticism might well be better than nothing and more helpful for some people than any traditional religion, but I think there is a middle ground between religions with too many boundaries and restrictions and religions without any, even within traditional forms such as Christianity.

Choice is not a religion. Spirituality is about limiting choice without limiting options, as we see in the lives of so many faithful people, whether Christian or Jewish or Muslim or Buddhist. The hermit moves into the desert. Moses leads the people of Israel out of Egypt. Jesus goes to the cross. Buddha sits under the bodhi tree and will not move until he knows. All of them had alternatives and tested other paths to enlightenment, but in the end they had few choices. In fact, they had only one choice–which ends up looking like no choice at all to the outsider.

The ethic that Jesus offers is not one of mindless self-denial or morbid anxiety. He states a fact, however, that most of us keep at bay: the spiritual life is not about acquiring more for ourselves but about giving up ourselves. Our compulsive buying, which is a sign of uncontrollable anxiety about our selves, reveals the paucity of our imagination as a culture. In fundamentally limiting the spiritual choices we have by thinking that they are as endlessly available as consumer goods, we smother the essential and simple truths. By insisting on the material and rational as the necessary components and measure of our reality, we eliminate the alternatives that are at the heart of religious practice. Oddly, this insistence is not absent from the "new age" religious syncretism I described above, even when someone professes belief in angels. The purpose of such spiritual practice, for many people, is material result: better health, more money, a long life, more possessions—not unlike the promise of *The Prayer of Jabez* and similar approaches to spiritual life. At the same time, we tend to insist that religion "make sense" the way an electrical system makes sense. It should be rational and understandable, with demonstrable benefits. We constrain the freedom of spirit that God freely gives us when we pile our closets high with material or spiritual goods. Paradoxically, endless choice limits our spiritual freedom.

As we grow toward wisdom, Jesus and all spiritual teachers say, we begin to focus on the essentials—if we are living in the Spirit, if we are living out our vocation. It is not a question of personal choice, which is why it also looks like no choice at all. This vocation in fact is not my own. I share it with others. And therefore I cannot unilaterally decide what to do with it. That is the essence of community that Jesus calls his followers to join.

Many reject the institutional church because they feel it constrains them now just as it did in their youth. What we are often running from, in fact, is a memory of church and not an experience of faith. It was unpleasant then, when we had to get up on Sunday morning and put on a suit and listen to someone talk about boring things that obviously our parents did not believe. It will be unpleasant now, this thinking goes, because nothing has changed. And these who have abandoned church might say: "Yes, that is exactly why I am not in the church, because of this attitude that I have to do what I'm told by some minister who has not lived my life. Or that you have to die for Jesus. Or for the church, worse yet. No thanks." The difference, however, is that we are no longer twelve year olds—except, it seems, when it comes to our faith.

All of us need to be seekers. We also need to be dwellers who stay in the tradition and keep the rituals. Seekers are constantly trying out something new. The two types do not often get along well in the same community. They do not understand that they are necessary partners without which nothing happens at all.

One might call Peter a seeker, the Beloved Disciple a dweller. One recognizes Jesus in contemplative quiet; the other impulsively goes to meet him. But in the end both live in the kingdom where, as Paul says, all things are possible for me but not all things are desirable. I need to be an adult in my spiritual life and that means making choices I can live with. I also need to recognize that the choices of others are not constrained by mine. Community, as I have said earlier, requires that my boundaries be permeable.

Jesus speaks to Peter the truth that is fundamental for everyone's spiritual future: "When you grow old, you will stretch out your hands, and someone else will fasten a belt around you and take you where you do not wish to go." In the end, I will lose all choice, as I understand it, because I will die—just as that brown trout died, suddenly and brutally and mindlessly, simply for being itself. Despite our professed belief that Jesus has conquered death, most Christians do not have an evolved attitude toward death. We avoid it. We want to postpone and/or manage the end of life with medications and machinery. We do not want to experience our own death as part of life. We do not want to suffer. All of these attitudes are contrary to what we see in the death and resurrection of Jesus. All of them deny that we are living a life after the death of death. No matter how often we profess that in the death of Jesus death has died, few of us can live as if death did not matter. And yet we, with Peter, are called to do just that.

In my work as a volunteer chaplain with a hospital, I have spent a lot of time with people who are dying, with the dead, and with their families. One memorable week when I was on call during the head chaplain's absence I was summoned for ten deaths. Each was different. Each was unexpected. One young man died from a gunshot wound, and I had to find a way to comfort twenty relatives at midnight. An older man died of cancer; his wife did not want me to pray with her and her daughter (a seminary professor who did not want prayer either). They agreed, however, that I might say something. As I did, the widow began to weep in the knowledge that she could not control her life and failed to save his. Two or three of the dead were old men who lived alone in single-room-occupancy hotels. I was the only one who came to acknowledge that they had been alive at all. This work has made me aware that death is not something to fear: I have seen my own in the faces of others. And that, I think, is the key. In being with others as they die, we come to understand how we are part of the fabric of existence, which includes not only the living but the dead. If we do not know the dead, we cannot know the living nor our own lives.

My father was diagnosed with Parkinson's disease in his late sixties. It took awhile for us to understand what that meant, for him and for the family. Parkinson's insinuates itself into the body. It is easy to deny that anything is happening at all—or to believe that medication can fix the disease. Nothing can cure Parkinson's, however. Inexorably it consumes the one it inhabits, weakening the body through uncontrollable shaking that not only uses up energy but subdues the mind and will. It had the same effect on my mother, who was caring for him. My parents fought back, once they had accepted the diagnosis. They joined a support group and did their best to enhance the quality of his and their lives. They played golf as long as he was able—an effort further complicated by my father's having an artificial shoulder joint. They continued their normal routine and decided to live as long as they possibly could on their own. In the end, it became painful to watch them struggle to hold on to normality. I and my sisters did not always agree with their choices. We wished that they would move into an assisted living environment, mainly so that my mother would have some relief from her duties as his constant caregiver.

My father was a vigorous man who prided himself on his physical skills and appearance. He lifted weights in the basement and loved to play golf. Parkinson's was designed, it seemed, to take away from him exactly what he was most proud of. Toward the end of his life he was reduced to spending most of his time in a wheelchair or in bed. He had trouble feeding and dressing himself. His speech was slurred and his mental processes were confused. He heard what was not there and remembered what had never happened. But at the same time he became gentler and more affectionate as he became more dependent on others. He did not want to stop doing what he had always loved— playing golf, driving, exercising—and sometimes he got angry at us for, as he thought, preventing him from doing what he wanted to do. One day he stood in the open door of the garage, leaning on his walker, and looked intently at a couple of the old trees by the house. He said, "I think I'll get the chain saw and take them down." We stared at him and saw, mentally, a man with the shakes and a walker bearing a chain saw into the woods. It was not a pretty sight. But there was also something admirable in his determination.

Near the end of his life, he said to one of my sisters, as he sat in his wheelchair on the deck, "It wasn't supposed to be like this." He meant that his and my mother's retirement was to be a time of enjoyment, golf, travel: reward for the years of hard work. He had retired at an early age but had worked (often two jobs) hard. My mother had climbed the executive ladder from a mortgage loan department to executive vice president of the largest bank in Virginia. They had come from humble roots and had done well. They had lived as most people would like to live and retired to a large and comfortable home on several green acres of land.

I suppose that my father imagined they would both live to a dignified old age and die quietly in their sleep. He certainly did not anticipate incapacitation or extended suffering. That was not the plan. Most people, I think, have a similar vision of the end of their lives. Suffering is for others. The thinking might go: It is too bad that some people end up in nursing homes or are unable to care for themselves, but I do not expect to have to change what I do even as I age. Or at least, if I have to slow down, it will be in a lush Florida landscape close to everything I need, including those who love me.

At his funeral, we placed around the casket a number of photographs of him and my mother. They showed him as a young man, the two of them as a young and handsome couple. Everyone's favorite pictured dad on a large boulder swinging a lariat over his head. His stance is bold and exuberant. He can do anything! Below him is my mother, whom it appears he is about to lasso. Someone asked her, "Did he rope you and carry you off?" As all photographs do, this one spells out graphically the essential fact of all life: every moment is our last. And therefore every moment is the best we have. At that time in his life, my father could go wherever he wanted. But there came a time when he stretched out his hands to be led by others.

The death of Jesus, like the death of my father, is not a charade. It is not an abstract theological example. It is a fact of my life and yours. When Mary Magdalene goes to the tomb to pay her respects to the dead Jesus, she expects nothing more than a tomb that contains a body. She is on her way to visit a corpse and to mourn. Jesus was executed like any criminal. As others do in their grief, she was searching for the one who was lost, hoping perhaps to find him as he once was, alive and warm. The loved ones of those who die often feel that they might meet the dead in familiar places—at the dinner table, in a familiar restaurant. Mary may have hoped to see Jesus again, but she was not expecting to. The Resurrection affirms exactly what every grieving person wants: the return of the dead.

She did not believe that God made Jesus die, nor that Jesus chose death. He went where he did not wish to go, if we can believe his fervent prayer that the cup of suffering be taken from him. But in a sense, he had no choice. He might have run away, of course. He might have abandoned his vocation to bear witness. But he did not. And that is really the message here. That we have a vocation as Christians that profoundly limits and joyously expands our choices. We may not run away. There are sheep to be fed.

How do we understand this call to freedom that looks like bondage, like being carried where we do not want to go? One of the clearest examples I know is that of Dietrich Bonhoeffer, who in 1943 was arrested and imprisoned for his part in a plot to kill Hitler and in 1945 was executed at the age of thirty-nine.[2] As a young man Bonhoeffer came to Union Theological Seminary as a post-doctoral student and teacher in 1930, where he also discovered Harlem. Attending Abyssinian Baptist Church, he came to appreciate the liturgical rhythms and social witness of the black church. When he returned to Germany, he took with him the deeper awareness and hatred of racism that sharpened his critiques of German anti-Semitism. When Adolf Hitler became Reich Chancellor of Germany in 1933, with the support of many German Christians, Bonhoeffer criticized the rise of Fascism in a radio address that was terminated by the authorities in the middle of the broadcast. His opposition to the Reich led him to become pastor to the German Lutheran congregations in London between 1933 and 1935, although he continued to work in opposition to Hitler.

In 1935 Bonhoeffer returned to Germany to organize a seminary in exile for the Confessing Church. It was an experiment in alternative community. Nonetheless, a majority of Confessing Church pastors took an oath of allegiance to the Führer in 1938, and within months all Jewish businesses were liquidated. In the spring of 1939, Bonhoeffer returned to New York. The question he pondered as friends at Union worked to secure a position for him in the United States was this:

2. For some of what follows, I am indebted to Scott Holland's essay, "First We Take Manhattan, Then We Take Berlin: Bonhoeffer's New York," in *CrossCurrents* 50:3 (Fall 2000), 369-82.

"Will the church merely gather up those whom the wheel has crushed or will it prevent the wheel from crushing them?"[3] Before the summer was out, he decided to return to Berlin to join the active resistance to Hitler, feeling that he would have no right to participate in Germany's restoration after the war if he did not share in his country's agony.

Bonhoeffer described this decision in a subsequent letter to his friend and biographer Eberhard Bethge, basing it on his new understanding of the condition of "the outcast, the suspects, the maltreated, the powerless, the oppressed, the reviled—in short from the perspective of those who suffer."[4] His point is that we find ourselves through encounters with others and their life stories, those without whom we cannot know ourselves. In Bonhoeffer's life and work, we can trace this maturing spiritual understanding of the difference between the imitative forms of discipleship and the creative power of obligation that can lead to death. "When Christ calls a man," he wrote, "he bids him come and die." So for him Christianity was never a matter of intellectual theory, doctrine, or mystical emotion, but obedient action in everyday life. In maturity he became, as Jesus was, the man for others.

In 1943, Dietrich Bonhoeffer was arrested and imprisoned for taking part in a plan to kill Hitler; on April 9, 1945, he was executed, by special order of Heinrich Himmler. He was thirty-nine years old—and within two months, Dachau, where he died, was liberated by the Americans.

3. Ibid, p. 375.
4. Dietrich Bonhoeffer, *Letters and Papers from Prison, New Greatly Enlarged Edition*, ed. Eberhard Bethge (New York: Simon and Schuster, 1997), p. 17.

While in prison Bonhoeffer wrote a letter to Bethge that makes sense of the strange idea of freedom I have been pursuing in this chapter. It is what Peter finally discovers and what we are each called to learn before we die.

> I'm still discovering right up to this moment that it is only by living completely in this world that one learns to have faith. One must completely abandon any attempt to make something of oneself, whether it be a saint, or a converted sinner, or a churchman (a so-called priestly type!), a righteous man or an unrighteous one, a sick man or a healthy one. By this-worldliness I mean living unreservedly in life's duties, problems, successes and failures, experiences and perplexities. In so doing we throw ourselves completely into the arms of God, taking seriously, not our own sufferings, but those of God in the world—watching with Christ in Gethsemane.[5]

Following this letter, Bonhoeffer enclosed a poem he had written, "Stations on the Road to Freedom," which includes these lines that are reminiscent of Jesus' words to Peter on the beach:

> Your hands, so strong and active,
> are bound; in helplessness now you see your action
> is ended; you sigh in relief, your cause committing
> to stronger hands; so now you may rest contented.[6]

The One whom Bonhoeffer followed is the same as the One who speaks to Peter on the shore of Galilee of being bound in faithfulness in order to be set free.

5. Ibid., p. 370.
6. Ibid., p. 371

It is the deeply moving paradox of life that Peter exemplifies and Bonhoeffer embodied. So that we will not assume that only the great and saintly live in this order, my father too, "so strong and active," was bound by the very man he was and eventually set free within his chains to be himself. I saw that happen as his death approached, as he faced himself. He did not change so much as evolve in spirit. He became physically more ethereal as he lost weight, reflecting perhaps the lightening of being that finally allows us to go. All of us in the family advanced toward self-awareness through and with him. All deaths bring us closer to being ourselves.

Over the years I have found myself returning, often without expecting it, to Dietrich Bonhoeffer and the story of his life. I first read his book, *The Cost of Discipleship*, when I was a teenager and was deeply impressed then with his moral certainty and assertiveness. It was perhaps one of the first books I read that revealed to me the seriousness of religious faith. The story of Bonhoeffer's death was not as important for me as the passion with which he engaged life in faith. His book about intentional community, *Life Together*, insisted on confronting the limitations imposed by community and the freedom implicit in commitment. I have struggled all my life to find that equanimity that he seems to have understood in his bones. It is, I think, the fundamental challenge of faith.

Later in the same poem Bonhoeffer writes,

> Freedom, how long we have sought thee in discipline,
> action, and suffering; dying, we now may behold thee
> revealed in the Lord.

This is the same Lord who asks Peter to follow him, at the beginning of their ministry together and at the end of Peter's life. In fact, the invitation is always there in some way. It always raises the question, Where are you going? Earlier in the gospel, after telling Peter that he will deny him three times, Jesus goes on to reassure him, saying, "Do not let your hearts be troubled. . . . I go to prepare a place for you—I will come again and will take you to myself, so that where I am, there you may be also. And you know the way to the place where I am going." Thomas said to him, "Lord, we do not know where you are going. How can we know the way?" Jesus said to him, "I am the way, and the truth, and the life. No one comes to the Father except through me" (John 14:3–6).

But it is not so easy as that. The way is vexed, the truth uncertain, and in a world of many faiths it is increasingly hard to accept Jesus' saying, "No one comes to the Father except through me." Set free by the certainty of death and its window onto the eternal, we pause, looking out on what landscape, what road, what destination? Peter threw off his clothes and leapt into the lake when he realized that Jesus was standing there waiting. Then this same Jesus warns Peter of the cost of giving up his life for the good of others, promising him that if he follows Jesus, he will be taken unceremoniously to his death. Follow me and give up your options. Here are your new clothes. Stand still while I wrap them around you. Hold these nails and stretch out your arms.

Peter might be forgiven for thinking that he was not following but being dragged.

Chapter 6

"You Follow Me!"

20 Peter turned and saw the disciple whom Jesus loved following them; he was the one who had reclined next to Jesus at the supper and had said, "Lord, who is it that is going to betray you?" 21 When Peter saw him, he said to Jesus, "Lord, what about him?" 22 Jesus said to him, "If it is my will that he remain until I come, what is that to you? Follow me!" 23 So the rumor spread in the community that this disciple would not die. Yet Jesus did not say to him that he would not die, but, "If it is my will that he remain until I come, what is that to you?" 24 This is the disciple who is testifying these things and has written them, and we know that his testimony is true. 25 But there are also many other things that Jesus did; if every one of them were written down, I suppose that the world itself could not contain the books that would be written.

When he instructs Peter to follow him, where is Jesus going? And where did Jesus come from? Both of these questions recur in various forms in John's Gospel and fundamentally they ask who Jesus is. Yet these last verses of the gospel seem to be about much more mundane issues and petty jealousies. The chapter does not end so much as wander off. Its message, however, is very much that of the rest of the chapter, and for our purposes points to the final dimension of the journey toward wisdom: the maturity that helps us to live in the world. It is mundane because the end of our journey with Jesus is our own lives.

Jesus calls Peter to follow him, and immediately Peter wants to know about the one who is following *them*—the Beloved Disciple. His presence almost seems to annoy Peter, who sounds like an older brother who does not want the younger to join him among the adults. Peter is "bonding" with Jesus. They have been reconciled. Peter's sins are forgiven. Peter wants this moment. Recall too that the Beloved Disciple is the one whose intimacy with Jesus is so compellingly revealed during the Last Supper. I sense here that Peter wants to replace the Beloved Disciple as the one who is most intimate with Jesus. The question Peter asks is also about preferment or preference. Who is most favored among the disciples?

In asking "What about him?" Peter is questioning Jesus about a specific prophecy about the Beloved Disciple, who was also the founder of the Johannine community and the presumed author of the Gospel of John. This community believed that the Beloved Disciple would not die until the second coming of Christ—a sign of his favored place among Jesus' followers. But this effort to explain why the prophecy has failed implies that the disciple has already died, even though he and his theology still influence the communal life of his followers. The community of the Beloved Disciple is known to have had a unique form of governance and theology among the earliest groups of Christians; its insights are preserved in John's Gospel and in

Christian mystical tradition. But there seems to be no question here, in Chapter 21, that Peter is the presumed leader of the emerging church. Whether this final section of the chapter is about Peter's leadership or a particular community's resistance to his authority in the emerging church is not our primary concern, however. Peter's somewhat testy question leads to a response from Jesus that frames our sixth and final perspective on the development of spiritual wisdom.

Jesus' response is essentially this: Do not worry about others. Tend to yourself. *You* follow me. This attitude seems, at first, contrary to what we take to be Christian obligation. We are called, are we not, to assist others in finding the truth of Christ, to make sure that they do not fall into sin and error? Was that not the message of the dialogue Jesus and Peter have had about caring for the sheep? This passage now suggests that these others are not our responsibility, that our primary obligation is to our own spiritual journey. The path that Jesus calls us to walk is different for each of us. Yet it is not about radical individualism, a further splintering of creation. Nor is it about the issue of church leadership.

The mature spirituality that Jesus calls Peter to embrace is one that transcends the boundaries of personal preference and even belief, one enabling a spiritual growth that does not define or limit others. This path leads to absorption in what I am calling the wisdom of God, a place of grace beyond religion and denomination. Adulthood itself—the time of physical aging—is a kind of wisdom, allowing us to be secure in our beliefs while generous to the beliefs of others. My journey is my own, but I walk with others—including people of other faiths—whose journeys are also good, although different. The net of our collective experience does not break. For many Christians this dimension of the spiritual life is counter-intuitive. It goes against all that they have been taught about the primacy of the Christian revelation. We have been told that Christ is the only way. In fact, the Gospel of John says explicitly that Jesus is "the way, the truth, and the life," and that no one comes to God except through him.

This apparent identification of Jesus as the only way to God comes in response to a question from Thomas about where Jesus is going and how it is that the disciples are to know how to follow him (John 14:5). This exchange immediately follows Peter's assertion that he will lay down his life for Jesus, who says that on the contrary Peter will deny him. You cannot follow me now, he tells Peter. But then he goes on to assure the disciples that he goes to prepare a place for them: "And you know the way to the place where I am going" (John 13:36–14:7). The question, once again, is: Who is Jesus for the disciples and for us?

He is the way that reveals truth and life, in which we might understand how to live abundantly. This way is the way of wisdom, which Jesus in his life has exemplified. "Live like this" might be another way of saying, "Follow me." Some Christians have taken this passage to mean that there is no other faithful way to salvation except through belief in Jesus Christ. But it seems to me that this point of view is exactly the self-centered religion that Jesus opposed by the way he lived. He did not offer the blessed assurance of salvation as a reward for following him, but (as he makes clear in John 21) assurance that this way of life will lead, just as his own did, to death. Therefore, Jesus says, live your life with complete engagement. Catch fish, feed sheep, eat breakfast. Do not worry about what you cannot control, especially the life journeys of those walking with you. The way is not afterlife: it *is* life. And each of us has one way that is distinctively our own. Our task is to find it and live it. Nonetheless, Jesus does not offer a way that is walked in self-sufficiency. As I have argued in this book, the goal of faithful living in the Christian tradition is in fact community—but a community of strangers, not of relatives.

Wisdom has a specific meaning in Judeo-Christian tradition which I think is intrinsic to John's Gospel, and looking briefly at that tradition will help us understand what spiritual maturity might mean. An ancient way of speaking about Jesus identifies him as the Sophia Wisdom of God, described, for example, in the book of Ecclesiasticus:

> "Then the Creator of all things gave me a command,
> and my Creator chose the place for my tent.
> He said, 'Make your dwelling in Jacob,
> and in Israel receive your inheritance.'
> Those who eat of me will hunger for more,
> and those who drink of me will thirst for more.'"
> (24:8, 21)

Like Wisdom, Jesus is the one who has come from and returns to heaven. This is the key to understanding his identity in John. The hymn that opens John's Gospel makes this plain: "In the beginning was the Word, and the Word was with God, and the Word was God." Jesus is the pre-existing Word that was with God in the beginning, and all things came into being through him. This Word came to dwell among us, and "we have seen his glory, the glory as of a father's only

son, full of grace and truth" (1:14). This glory is manifest in the resurrected Jesus on the shore of Lake
Tiberias in John 21 and in the Shekinah seen by the
people of Israel in the Tent of Meeting. His life journey is like the pilgrimage of Wisdom, God's Spirit,
which is chronicled in the Wisdom of Solomon. The
author of John seems to have drawn on that apoc-
ryphal book, particularly Chapters 10 through 19.[1]

Jesus explicitly identifies himself with the figure of
Wisdom, which aided God's people in previous genera-
tions, providing water and manna in the wilderness, or
breakfast by the lake. Wisdom personified in the Hebrew
Scriptures now walks the earth in the form of Jesus (and
also became a way of talking about Torah for Jews). He
was not only speaking for God, he was the very embod-
iment of God's message in human form. This is a dar-
ing (and if you are Jewish offensive) concept, that Jesus
is the human form of an attribute of God's Wisdom.

In Proverbs 9:1–6, Wisdom is personified for the
first time in Hebrew scripture and, perhaps surprisingly, is clearly depicted as a woman:

Wisdom has built her house, . . .
she has mixed her wine,
she has also set her table.
She has sent out her servant-girls,
she calls from the highest places in the town,
"You that are simple, turn in here!"
To those without sense she says,

1. In what follows, I have drawn on the insights of Ben Witherington III,
Jesus the Sage: The Pilgrimage of Wisdom (Minneapolis, MN: Fortress Press,
1989), particularly here pp. 370-80. The idea that Jesus is the Wisdom of
God is not a new one; early Christologies drew on the Wisdom imagery
of Israel. See also Gerhard von Rad's *Wisdom in Israel* (Valley Forge, PA:
Trinity Press International, 1993).

"Come, eat of my bread
and drink of the wine I have mixed.

Lay aside immaturity, and live,
and walk in the way of insight."

The echoes in Jesus' ministry, especially in the eucharistic imagery, are clear. But never in Israel had Wisdom been identified with a particular person, as it is with Jesus in the gospels.[2] He spoke as Wisdom in binding his disciples to himself personally, and we have seen that John's Gospel reflects that personal closeness. This radical departure from Jewish tradition was taken up in the early church as part of its earliest efforts to understand the meaning of Jesus' life and ministry; for example, Jesus is a sage, or Wisdom figure, in the so-called "sayings gospel" embedded in Matthew, Mark, and Luke. Even before the gospels were written, Paul told the Corinthians that God "is the source of your life in Christ Jesus, who became for us wisdom from God" (1 Cor. 1:30). More extravagantly, in the letter to the Colossians he calls Jesus

the image of the invisible God, the firstborn of all creation; for in him all things in heaven and on earth were created, things visible and invisible, whether thrones or dominions or rulers or powers—all things have been created through him and for him. He himself is before all things, and in him all things hold together. He is the head of the body, the church; he is the beginning, the firstborn from the dead, so that he might come to have first place in everything (1:15–18).

2. The idea of Jesus as Wisdom turns up not only in John but in other gospels: Matt. 11:19, 28-30, 12:42 and Luke 21:15, to name a few places.

Although Jesus is not explicitly named as Wisdom in Colossians and similar texts (see Philippians 2:5–11), his attributes are like those of Wisdom and echo earlier Jewish wisdom hymns. Drawing on this tradition enabled early Christians to describe what they saw as Christ's divinity in terms that did not violate their belief in one God.

In John's Gospel the "I am" sayings—where Jesus calls himself the living bread, the light of the world, the door, life, and the true vine—are derived from attributes of personified Wisdom in Israel's tradition.[3] The point of these sayings in John (and the point of the gospel itself) is that *all the believer needs can be found in Jesus.* That is the same message as in the Wisdom literature, except that here it is applied to Jesus rather than Wisdom. Our destiny hangs on whether we accept or reject Jesus, the Wisdom of God. The author of the Wisdom of Solomon wrote, "Who has learned your counsel, unless you have given wisdom and sent your holy spirit from on high? And thus the paths of those on earth were set right, and people were taught what pleases you, and were saved by wisdom" (Wis. 9:17–18). According to John, salvation comes from the indwelling Christ—from the deeply organic relationship symbolized by the vine and branches—just as Wisdom itself was perceived as a path of salvation.

For the author of John, understanding the pilgrimage of Wisdom is essential to understanding who Jesus is. The gospel concludes with Jesus, the Wisdom figure, who leaves his final teaching with his disciples and then disappears. When he says to Peter, "Follow

3. See John 6:35, 51; 8:12; 10:7,9,11,14; 11:25; 14:6; 15:1,5.

me," however, what does Jesus mean? Once again, the question is: Where is he going?

But for the disciples and for us, the question is: Where do *we* come from and where are we going? Jesus disappears at the end of John 21 into a virtual library of possibilities ("But there are also many other things that Jesus did; if every one of them were written down, I suppose that the world itself could not contain the books that would be written.") Who are we following? Where? These questions are about who we are, as they are also about the identities of Peter and the Beloved Disciple. Another way to phrase this message is: Don't worry about who someone else is. Know who you are. The journey and its end are self-awareness.

This question is a practical one about daily living, as this last section of John 21 also returns to common concerns. The Wisdom of the Hebrew scriptures—and indeed the wisdom tradition in all religions—is about right living, which assumes a right relationship with God (or with the Absolute in nontheistic traditions). One simple example is Proverbs 8:32–36, where we read:

> And now, my children, listen to me:
> happy are those who keep my ways.
> Hear instruction and be wise, and do not neglect it.
> Happy is the one who listens to me,
> watching daily at my gates,
> waiting beside my doors.
> For whoever finds me, finds life
> and obtains favor from the LORD.
> But those who miss me injure themselves;
> all who hate me love death.

The speaker, personified Wisdom, is thought of as immanent in the world: "The LORD by wisdom founded the earth," according to Proverbs 3:19. This tradition calls humans to life in the most concrete terms. It concerns itself primarily with the issues of meaning in ordinary existence. Although there are mystical aspects to the wisdom perspective—and the Wisdom of Solomon points toward a trinitarian concept of godhead—at heart it is about living on earth. It is a call to be present.

Jesus may be the Wisdom of God in biblical tradition, but that is mere academic knowledge if we do not come to know him as the wisdom of our own lives. The fundamental question is: Who is Christ for us?

At one point in his letters from prison Dietrich Bonhoeffer wrote that "we are moving towards a completely religionless time; people as they are now simply cannot be religious any more." He did not live to develop the idea fully, and there has been a lot of speculation about what he meant. He does suggest later in this letter that the Western form of Christianity might be "only a preliminary stage to a complete absence of religion"—and if so, "what is a religionless Christianity?" [4] There is a clue here to the meaning of Christ for us today that is probably not exactly what Bonhoeffer had in mind, but I think it is provocatively close: religion represents the conceptual, even mythological, perspective that has produced and nourished the institutional church as the vehicle for Christ's presence in the world. The wisdom tradition suggests, to the contrary, that Christ as God's Wisdom can be directly revealed to us as the way of our lives. Now we see, as Paul said, face to face. In Jesus, we learn who we are in our deepest selves, where God dwells with us. As

4. Bonhoeffer, *Letters*, 279-80.

Jesus demonstrated in his life, we become enlightened human beings when the human and the divine dwell intimately together.

On the shore of Lake Tiberias Jesus speaks directly to the situation of Peter and the disciples in the boat. He gives them practical advice on how to live: Put down your nets over there. Come and eat breakfast. Feed my sheep. Follow me. Don't worry about someone else's relationship to me but get on with your life. Do not assume that you can control your future.

Jesus calls the disciples to the world and to the present. This is the work of the spirit, to renew the earth, *this* earth on which we walk every day. It is the meaning of the resurrection as well.

The way of wisdom is not fundamentally about redemption from the cares and problems of the world, nor a ticket to some better world beyond the grave. Jesus *comes back* from death to reclaim the present for God's Holy Spirit. He comes back not to take Peter and the Beloved Disciple out of the world but to send them back into it, although transformed by Christ's presence with them (a definitive sign of God's commitment to human life). There is no escape from the work of the day in the realm of the eternal. Jesus himself makes that clear when he drinks the earthly cup. The point of his life is not his death, nor even the crucifixion, which is after all simply another (particularly brutal) example of everyone's end. The point of his life is his life. Where you are right now and what you are doing right now is the meaning of life.

At the beginning of this chapter in John, Peter goes fishing—returns to the world—to take up his former way of life. That is simply not possible, however, as he soon discovers. It is not possible because the world has been transformed in his experience now by the presence of the resurrected Jesus. The old world has died. If he goes back to it, he will die. Of course, he will also die if he follows Jesus, but the deaths are of radically different importance. In following Jesus, he dies into life. The example of Jesus transforms his perspective so that he can go where engagement, not escape, awaits him. Peter takes up the tasks of ministry, as I said in the previous chapter, on behalf of others. What matters here is the individual's encounter with the compelling wisdom of God's powerlessness in the world. It is that powerlessness that most deeply engages the person of faith. In Judaism, the concept of *tikkun olam*[5] offers a similar perspective. In creation, God has been splintered into the world that cannot be restored except by the work of the faithful community. The work of human life is restoration: acts of compassion in community. That brings us closer to God than we were before because it makes us more like God.

God's wisdom is embodied in the local gathering of faithful people, as it is in the individual spirit. God's wisdom is manifest in our lives. That is the message Jesus has for Peter in John 21 and for us as we grow to spiritual maturity. It is the message of mature faith. Grand systems are not as helpful as the experience of individuals with others. New models of the church are being born every day, many of them meeting in community on week nights to sing and pray—sometimes with Scripture, sometimes without texts at all, or with non-canonical texts such as the

---

5. The meaning of this Hebrew phrase is "to repair the world," seen by Jews as the task of humankind. This idea has particular importance in Kabbalah and Jewish mysticism. See George Robinson, *Essential Judaism: A Complete Guide to Beliefs, Customs, and Rituals* (New York: Simon and Schuster Pocket Books, 2000), pp. 373-84.

Gospel of Thomas, sometimes with the works of poets and writers who may or may not be Christian.

Spiritual wisdom, in individuals as well as in the Church, is about developing a greater tolerance for differences within and without. Because of my former work as the editor of an interreligious journal, where my assistant editor was Jewish, I was constantly aware of the crude image of the church militant that has brought suffering to many. We have not always been kind to strangers. The catch of the great variety of fish in John 21, as well as Jesus' comment to Peter at the end of the chapter, suggest to me that we might be more open to variety and leave the sorting out of the acceptable and the unacceptable to God, which is where such sortings properly belong. Let the weeds grow in the garden, Jesus says in one of his parables (Matt. 13:24–30). We can pluck them out later. Who knows which of these plants is a weed before the time of harvest? Perhaps there are no weeds.

If we live in our vocation to bear witness, keep our spiritual practice, embrace *metanoia* in community, and do the work of reconciliation, we can die in strength and let others live in peace. That seems to me the work and wisdom of spiritual maturity. Some have called this age the time of the Holy Spirit, when the institution of the church will be changed into a new community of the faithful that is less concerned with orthodoxies and more with the poverty and sickness of the world that may kill us all if we cannot become healers. Bonhoeffer offered a perspective on the nature of this future church, which may also offer another insight into what he might have meant by "religionless Christianity." He wrote that "the church is the church only when it exists for others. . . . It must not underestimate the importance of human example (which has its origin in the humanity of Jesus . . .); it is not abstract argument, but example, that gives its word emphasis and power."[6] This, I believe, is the way of wisdom.

In the end Jesus says, "Follow me." Follow my example. Do what I have done. That is also what he says in the beginning. Following him means giving up our lives and prerogatives to live as Christians who have already died. It means following him into God's larger wisdom, where others can live as well. That wisdom is larger than all of our ways. Ultimately, I think that we are called to live in this sixth dimension of wisdom, and the church is called to the same vocation. It is being called to radical discipleship in the world, not beyond it. If we follow Jesus in this journey, as he is revealed to us in this chapter from John, we see before us a way of living together as Christians that is potentially healing and also fertile. We can grow together in such rich soil. These are dimensions of spiritual life—manifestations of adult faith in community—that sustained the church in its early years and can sustain us now. In the world, it may mean giving up the notion of a united faith, allowing others to find their way to God's wisdom in their own time. As Jesus says, what is that to us?

This more limited understanding of the church is, I think, a more mature vision, one that grows organically out of initial isolation and discernment through transforming encounter with the divine and becomes, in time, a vehicle for changing the lives of others through service to them, even it if means giving up our precious selves. We all begin this journey in faith in the same way, like those isolated disciples, naked, in a boat

6. Bonhoeffer, *Letters*, 382-8

on the Sea of Tiberias trying to figure out who is standing on the shore and what he is telling them to do. The
church has never really been anything else.

For a number of years, when I still lived in Pennsylvania, I took a day off from work on my birthday to go
fishing. Since I was born on March 29, the day has often
been cold—and once even snowy—but it was something
I did as a ritual that reconnected me to myself. I have
seldom caught fish on my birthday. At the beginning of
this book I recounted the story of my birthday fishing
trip to Lake Arenal in Costa Rica, a sign of my spiritual
isolation at that time of my life. Following that trip and
a move to New York City, I allowed the tradition to
lapse. The ostensible reason was that I did not have a
car and the expense of renting one seemed dispropor-
tionate. But the truth was rooted in that same spiritual
condition that afflicted the disciples at the beginning of
their journey to the Risen Jesus and wisdom. I was dis-
connected from my own life-giving waters.

In the years since I made that trip to Costa Rica, I
have discerned my own call to vocation in community
and been changed in the experience of meeting Jesus
regularly in the eucharist. Working in hospitals as a
volunteer chaplain, and with seekers as a spiritual director, has taught me to feed others. In ordination to the
diaconate I have allowed myself to be bound and led
along a path that as yet has no discernible terminus,
except my own death.

When I turned fifty-seven, I realized that it was
time to go fishing on my birthday again. It was the first
such trip since Arenal. As then, I went to a place I had
never fished before. My father had died two months
before, midway through a year that included several

other life-altering and sometimes stressful events. I needed to go fishing. I also understood that the person who was packing his gear for the day was not the same one who had flown in despair to Costa Rica in 1994. This was a trip taken in hope. I knew more about myself and in less than a month would marry a woman who had brought to my life transforming love.

The river I decided to fish was the Connetquot, located about halfway out on Long Island. It runs through a large wildlife preserve, and I had heard that it was an extraordinary river for trout, as well as a beautiful place to be. Unlike most trout streams in the United States, you "rent" a stretch of the Connetquot for a half or whole day and have exclusive use of the one-hundred-yard section for that period.

The day was cool and overcast, with an expected high temperature of only forty-five degrees and a chance of showers. I had reserved an afternoon slot to take advantage of whatever mid-day warmth there might be, but still packed a sweater, jacket, and thick insulated socks. When the sections of the river were assigned to the waiting anglers, I received one that several of the veterans assured me was a good "beat" (as such parcels of a stream are called). I put on my chest-high waders, fishing vest containing dozens of different artificial flies and lures, my broad-brimmed Tilley hat, and sunglasses. After stringing up my rod, I started off along the dirt path that paralleled the river up to my beat. Another angler walked along with me and told me about the rules of fishing the stream.

Fly fishers approach trout in two ways: one is by floating bushy flies on top of the water; the other is by drifting nymphs (insect larva imitations) along the bottom. The fish "come up" for surface lures when insects are hatching—when they are emerging from their larval forms on the surface or when they are mating and touching down briefly to lay eggs. This kind of surface fishing—known as dry fly fishing—is the most exciting because one can see the fish actively feeding. Nymph fishing is more subtle. It is rare to see the fish one is trying to catch—or, if one does see the fish, it is almost impossible to see the nymph as it drifts along. The fish move as they feed and it is difficult to tell if they are striking one's unseen lure. Nymphing is more like work than dry-fly fishing. But catching a fish on a nymph is the more mystical path.

My companion told me that anglers are forbidden to add weight—usually in the form of small tin or lead balls—to the line in order to put a nymph on the bottom where the fish feed. Given the time of year, I assumed that I would be nymphing for most of the day. This new information was somewhat dismaying, since it is difficult to sink an unweighted nymph. I am also not a very good nymph fisherman. Like most, I prefer to fish on the surface.

One cannot catch fish with nymphs unless the lure is literally bouncing or dragging along the bottom of the stream. Feeling that movement is the angler's first challenge. The next is to feel the trout's mouth on the lure. Trout know instantly when they taste the artificial bug and spit it right out. The angler has only an instant to tighten the line and hook the fish. Nymphing is either frustrating or meditative. Catching fish in this way is as much about the stillness of one's mind as it is about anything else.

My way of fishing, however, has been to roam up and down a stream, frequently changing flies, trying out new ideas. I have been as restless on the water as

I am in the rest of my life. As I looked into the depths of my beat on the Connetquot, I feared that I was in for a long day of catching no fish. I tied on two nymphs, one on the main line and one on a length of line known as a dropper, in order to add weight legally and to increase my chances of attracting fish. Two lures are better than one. I could see trout lined up in the center of the stream. That was encouraging.

I began to cast methodically, throwing the line upstream and holding my rod high and parallel to the surface so that the line remained taut and the nymphs sank toward the bottom. Theoretically, by the time they were deep enough, they would be in front of the hungry trout. And so it was. It seemed remarkably easy, as if I had suddenly learned everything I needed to know about nymph fishing. I was confident that the nymphs I had tied on my line were good choices. I could see the fish feeding. On the third or fourth pass, I caught a fish.

My daughter once asked me how I knew when a fish took a nymph, and I replied that I just knew. When it works, it works. There is a moment as the nymph is drifting downstream when the line comes alive. It is a slight hesitation, an odd sense of counter motion, conveyed almost telepathically from the depths of the stream to the angler's nervous system. The arm jerks. The fish is on. It comes up struggling from the bottom, emerging first as motion and then as color. It may run to find shelter under the bank and beneath a fallen tree. One may not actually see the fish until it is finally brought to the net. All of this happens in the self not in the mind. It is nonthinking. And I had never felt that state of emptiness so deeply as I did that day.

I fished that day as I have never fished before, catching fish with ease, as if each time I cast I knew exactly where they were even when I could not see them. On one cast, I caught two fish at once, one on each of the nymphs. Like the disciples in the boat on Galilee, my net was filled to overflowing, even though I released all the fish. The abundance of the water revealed itself, even though the day got progressively colder and at one point in the afternoon there was the brief advertised shower. Whereas in the past, my birthday excursions were barren, I suddenly knew where to seek the fish. No one was standing on the shore directing me to drop my nymph in one place or another, but within I felt that same assurance of purpose and direction. Unlike Arenal, I had no guide who knew the water. The water and I knew each other.

This experience is a rendering of what I mean when I talk about the way of wisdom as the living of one's life. It comes from practice—in the case of fly fishing, the practice of fishing, but in spiritual terms, the practice of one's life in the divine. This practice in both cases is about paying attention, being mindful, and leaving behind the self that always insists on its own way. The way of wisdom is about being united with the one who leads the way, which is the way itself. Having the clear mind necessary for this work is also the result of consciously coming to terms with others on our way and with our own past. This clarity often comes from stressful life events, in my case beginning with the loss of my job and family in the early 1990s. Death is often not too far away, as it was for the disciples and as it was for me on the Connetquot. My father's death had cleared the way for me, not because he had been in the way but because

I had been in my way. His death has introduced me to the final barrier of my own life.

My father was not a fisherman, and I was not consciously thinking about him while I fished on my birthday. But I know that his death changed me, not only as all deaths change us when we encounter them, but more deeply (because he was my father) called into question and into being who I am. Seeing who we are in this way also helps us to get over ourselves, to leave the obstructing self behind—the one we create for protection. In dying and returning, Jesus also shows us that dying to the self is not about disappearing so much as it is about being transformed. What matters is how we go on with our lives. What matters is only life and death and how we come to terms with what is in fact one entity. Death and life are actually one, and the way of wisdom runs through it, as Jesus makes explicit in his living and dying.

During the day on the Connetquot I caught twelve fish, a good mystical number that makes more sense to me than the one hundred and fifty-three caught by the disciples. The last fish I caught came at about 4:00 PM. The temperature had dropped to about thirty-five degrees. I was shivering—a sign of hypothermia—and I knew that I had to get out of the water soon. But I also felt the need to catch one more fish—to reach that number twelve—and I cast upstream toward the end of a fallen tree that I knew from earlier in the afternoon was harboring a very large fish. On my first cast, I felt a more pronounced than usual tug that sharply tightened the line. The fish had me. It moved slowly out from under the log, as if it were in control of the moment, and made a quick run downstream toward rocks that would have surely snapped my line. I turned it toward the shore, giving it almost no room to maneuver. My rod was bent into a full half circle. I could see the fish below the surface darting back and forth. Its back broke the surface. It jumped, standing a moment on its brilliantly colored tail. And then I held him in my hands over the water. This fish weighed about five pounds. It was at least twenty inches in length. A good fish, we say. The best fish of the day. The twelfth fish. I was finished. There were no other fish to catch.

It is a moment of unsurpassable grace, when we hold what we need in our hands.

The search for direction is like that. One works at the practice of the Spirit. One does the work of wisdom. The large fish is where it should be and, in time, reveals itself. At the *kairos* moment, we have the skills to see it. When it is in our hands, we are called to feed others with it, to show them how the Spirit moves with us toward understanding. In the way of wisdom is who we are called to be. It is not a destination. Along the way, we will find fish like that large one I took from the Connetquot. We carry them with us, colors still vibrant, along the shore, walking purposefully in the company of the disciples, who are carrying all one hundred and fifty-three of their fish too. I give mine to my father, to you, to anyone who needs them. We give them all away, these brilliant fish of our being. The faithful community is just like that.

Sources

Barnstone, Willis, ed., *The Other Bible: Jewish Pseude-pigrapha, Christian Apocrypha, Gnostic Scriptures, Kabbalah, Dead Sea Scrolls.* New York: HarperSan-Francisco, 1984.

Bonhoeffer, Dietrich, *Discipleship*, Dietrich Bonhoeffer Works, Volume 4. Minneapolis: Fortress Press, 2001.

Bonhoeffer, Dietrich, *Letters and Papers from Prison*, New Greatly Enlarged Edition. Edited by Eberhard Bethge. New York: Simon and Schuster, 1997.

Brown, Raymond E., (introduction, translation, and notes), *The Anchor Bible. The Gospel According to John* (2 volumes). Garden City, NY: Doubleday and Company, 1966.

Brown, Raymond E., *The Community of the Beloved Disciple: The Life, Loves, and Hates of an Individual Church in New Testament Times.* New York: Paulist Press, 1979.

Brown, Raymond E., Joseph A. Fitzmyer, S.J., Roland E. Murphy, O.Carm., eds. *The New Jerome Biblical Commentary*. Englewood Cliffs, NJ: Prentice Hall, 1990.

Greenacre, Roger, and Jeremy Haselock, *The Sacrament of Easter*. Grand Rapids, MI: Wm. B. Eerdmans Publishing Co., 1995.

Heschel, Abraham Joshua, *The Sabbath*. New York: Farrar, Straus and Giroux, 1951, 1979.

Howard-Brook, Wes, *Becoming Children of God: John's Gospel and Radical Discipleship*. Maryknoll, NY: Orbis Books, 1994.

Howard-Brook, Wes, *The Church Before Christianity*. Maryknoll, NY: Orbis Books, 2001.

Kierkegaard, Soren, *The Sickness Unto Death: A Christian Psychological Exposition for Upbuilding and Awakening*. Edited and translated by Howard V. Hong and Edna H. Hong. Princeton: Princeton University Press, 1980.

Leach, Edmund, "Fishing for Men on the Edge of the Wilderness," Robert Alter and Frank Kermode, eds., *The Literary Guide to the Bible*. Cambridge, MA: Belknap Press, Harvard University Press, 1987.

Nouwen, Henri J.M., *The Wounded Healer: Ministry in Contemporary Society*. New York: Doubleday Image Books, 1990.

Robinson, George, *Essential Judaism: A Complete Guide to Beliefs, Customs, and Rituals*. New York: Simon and Schuster Pocket Books, 2000.

St. John of the Cross, Kieran Kavanaugh, O.C.D. and Otilio Rodriguez, O.C.D., trans., *The Collected Works of St. John of the Cross*. Washington, DC: ICS Publications, Institute of Carmelite Studies, 1979.

Von Rad, Gerhard, *Wisdom in Israel*. Valley Forge, PA: Trinity Press International, 1972.

Wilkinson, Bruce, *The Prayer of Jabez: Breaking Through to the Blessed Life*. Sisters, OR: Multnomah Publishers, 2000.

Witherington III, Ben, *Jesus the Sage: The Pilgrimage of Wisdom*. Minneapolis, MN: Fortress Press, 1994.

Zornberg, Avivah Gottlieb,. *The Particulars of Rapture: Reflections on Exodus*. New York: Doubleday, 2001.